2ⁿᵈ EDITION

Ventures

STUDENT'S BOOK

BASIC

Gretchen Bitterlin   Dennis Johnson   Donna Price   Sylvia Ramirez

K. Lynn Savage (Series Editor)

CAMBRIDGE
UNIVERSITY PRESS

CAMBRIDGE
UNIVERSITY PRESS

One Liberty Plaza, 20th Floor, New York, NY 10006, USA

Cambridge University Press is part of the University of Cambridge.

It furthers the University's mission by disseminating knowledge in the pursuit of education, learning and research at the highest international levels of excellence.

www.cambridge.org
Information on this title: www.cambridge.org/9781107641020

© Cambridge University Press 2014

First published 2008
9th printing 2016

Printed in Italy by Rotolito Lombarda S.p.A.

A catalogue record for this publication is available from the British Library

ISBN 978-1-107-64102-0 Student's Book with Audio CD
ISBN 978-1-107-69108-7 Workbook with Audio CD
ISBN 978-1-139-88532-4 Online Workbook
ISBN 978-1-107-67608-4 Teacher's Edition with Audio CD / CD-ROM
ISBN 978-1-107-66806-5 Class Audio CDs
ISBN 978-1-107-61622-6 Presentation Plus

Additional resources for this publication at www.cambridge.org/ventures

Art direction, book design, photo research, and layout services: Q2A / Bill Smith
Audio production: CityVox, LLC

Authors' acknowledgments

The authors would like to acknowledge and thank focus group participants and reviewers for their insightful comments, as well as Cambridge University Press editorial, marketing, and production staffs, whose thorough research and attention to detail have resulted in a quality product.

The publishers would also like to extend their particular thanks to the following reviewers and consultants for their valuable insights and suggestions:

Kit Bell, LAUSD division of Adult and Career Education, Los Angeles, CA; **Bethany Bogage**, San Diego Community College District, San Diego, CA; **Leslie Keaton Boyd**, Dallas ISD, Dallas, TX; **Barbara Brodsky**, Teaching Work Readiness English for Refugees – Lutheran Family Services, Omaha, NE; **Jessica Buchsbaum**, City College of San Francisco, San Francisco, CA; **Helen Butner**, University of the Fraser Valley, British Columbia, Canada; **Sharon Churchill Roe**, Acadia University, Wolfville, NS, Canada; **Lisa Dolehide**, San Mateo Adult School, San Mateo, CA; **Yadira M. Dominguez**, Dallas ISD, Dallas, TX; **Donna M. Douglas**, College of DuPage, Glen Ellyn, IL; **Latarsha Dykes**, Broward Collge, Pembroke Pines, FL; **Megan L. Ernst**, Glendale Community College, Glendale, CA; **Megan Esler**, Portland Community College, Portland, OR; **Jennifer Fadden**, Fairfax County Public Schools, Fairfax, VA; **Fotine Fahouris**, College of Marin, Kentfield, CA; **Lynn Francis, M.A, M.S.**, San Diego Community College, San Diego, CA; **Danielle Gines**, Tarrant County College, Arlington, TX; **Katherine Hayne**, College of Marin, Kentfield, CA; **Armenuhi Hovhannes**, City College of San Francisco, San Francisco, CA; **Fayne B. Johnson**; **Martha L. Koranda**, College of DuPage, Glen Ellyn, IL; **Daphne Lagios**, San Mateo Adult School, San Mateo, CA; **Judy Langelier**, School District of Palm Beach County, Wellington, FL; **Janet Les**, Chilliwack Community Services, Chilliwack, British Columbia, Canada; **Keila Louzada**, Northern Virginia Community College, Sterling, VA; **Karen Mauer**, Fort Worth ISD, Fort Worth, TX; **Silvana Mehner**, Northern Virginia Community College, Sterling, VA; **Astrid T. Mendez-Gines,** Tarrant County College, Arlington, TX; **Beverly A. Miller**, Houston Community College, Houston, TX; **José Montes, MS. Ed.**, The English Center, Miami-Dade County Public Schools, Miami, FL; **Suzi Monti**, Community College of Baltimore County, Baltimore, MD; **Irina Morgunova**, Roxbury Community College, Roxbury Crossing, MA; **Julia Morgunova**, Roxbury Community College, Roxbury Crossing, MA; **Susan Otero**, Fairfax County Public Schools, Fairfax, VA; **Sergei Paromchik**, Hillsborough County Public Schools, Tampa, FL; **Pearl W. Pigott**, Houston Community College, Houston, TX; **Marlene Ramirez**, The English Center, Miami-Dade County Public Schools, Miami, FL; **Cory Rayala**, Harbor Service Center, LAUSD, Los Angeles, CA; **Catherine M. Rifkin**, Florida State College at Jacksonville, Jacksonville, FL; **Danette Roe**, Evans Community Adult School, Los Angeles, CA; **Maria Roy**, Kilgore College, Kilgore, TX; **Jill Shalongo**, Glendale Community College, Glendale, CA, and Sierra Linda High School, Phoenix, AZ; **Laurel Owensby Slater**, San Diego Community College District, San Diego, CA; **Rheba Smith**, San Diego Community College District, San Diego, CA; **Jennifer Snyder**, Portland Community College, Portland, OR; **Mary K. Solberg**, Metropolitan Community College, Omaha, NE; **Rosanne Vitola**, Austin Community College, Austin, TX

Scope and sequence

UNIT TITLE TOPIC	FUNCTIONS	LISTENING AND SPEAKING	VOCABULARY	GRAMMAR FOCUS
Welcome pages 2–5	■ Identifying the letters of the alphabet ■ Spelling names ■ Identifying classroom directions ■ Identifying numbers	■ Saying classroom directions ■ Saying the alphabet ■ Saying numbers	■ Classroom directions ■ The alphabet with capital and lowercase letters ■ Numbers	
Unit 1 **Personal information** pages 6–17 Topic: **Describing people**	■ Identifying names ■ Identifying area codes and phone numbers ■ Identifying countries of origin ■ Exchanging personal information	■ Asking and answering questions about personal information	■ Personal information ■ Countries ■ Months of the year	■ Possessive adjectives (*my, your, his, her*)
Unit 2 **At school** pages 18–29 Topic: **The classroom**	■ Identifying classroom objects ■ Describing location ■ Finding out location	■ Asking what someone needs ■ Asking about and giving the location of things	■ Classroom furniture ■ Classroom objects ■ Days of the week	■ Prepositions of location (*in, on, under*)
Review: Units 1 and 2 pages 30–31		■ Understanding conversations		
Unit 3 **Friends and family** pages 32–43 Topic: **Family**	■ Identifying family relationships ■ Describing a family picture	■ Asking and answering questions about family relationships	■ Family relationships ■ Family members ■ People	■ *Yes / No* questions with *have*
Unit 4 **Health** pages 44–55 Topic: **Health problems**	■ Describing health problems	■ Asking and answering questions about health problems	■ The doctor's office ■ Body parts ■ Health problems	■ Singular and plural nouns
Review: Units 3 and 4 pages 56–57		■ Understanding conversations		
Unit 5 **Around town** pages 58–69 Topic: **Places and locations**	■ Identifying buildings and places ■ Describing location	■ Asking and answering questions about where someone is ■ Asking and answering questions about the location of buildings and places ■ Describing your neighborhood	■ Buildings and places ■ Transportation	■ Prepositions of location (*on, next to, across from, between*) ■ *Where* questions

READING	WRITING	LIFE SKILLS	PRONUNCIATION
■ Reading classroom directions ■ Reading the alphabet ■ Reading numbers	■ Writing the alphabet ■ Writing numbers	■ Understanding classroom directions	■ Pronouncing the alphabet ■ Pronouncing numbers
■ Reading a paragraph about a new student	■ Completing sentences giving personal information ■ Completing an ID card	■ Reading an ID card	■ Pronouncing key vocabulary ■ Pronouncing area codes and phone numbers
■ Reading a note about school supplies ■ Reading a memo about class information	■ Completing sentences about class information	■ Reading a class schedule	■ Pronouncing key vocabulary
			■ Pronouncing *a* as in *name* and *o* as in *phone*
■ Reading a paragraph about a family	■ Completing sentences about a family ■ Completing sentences about your family	■ Reading a housing application	■ Pronouncing key vocabulary
■ Reading a paragraph about a visit to the doctor's office	■ Completing a sign-in sheet at the doctor's office	■ Reading a label on a box of medicine	■ Pronouncing key vocabulary
			■ Pronouncing *e* as in *read, i* as in *five,* and *u* as in June
■ Reading a notice about a library opening ■ Reading a description of someone's street	■ Completing sentences describing your street	■ Reading a map	■ Pronouncing key vocabulary

UNIT TITLE TOPIC	FUNCTIONS	LISTENING AND SPEAKING	VOCABULARY	GRAMMAR FOCUS
Unit 6 **Time** pages 70–81 Topic: **Daily activities and time**	■ Asking the time ■ Asking for and giving information about the days and times of events	■ Asking and answering questions about the time ■ Asking and answering questions about events	■ Clock time ■ Activities and events ■ Times of the day	■ *Yes / No* questions with *be*
Review: Units 5 and 6 pages 82–83		■ Understanding conversations		
Unit 7 **Shopping** pages 84–95 Topic: **Clothes and prices**	■ Identifying clothing items ■ Reading prices ■ Identifying colors	■ Asking and answering questions about prices ■ Identifying the colors of clothing	■ Clothing ■ Prices ■ Colors	■ *How much is? / How much are?*
Unit 8 **Work** pages 96–107 Topic: **Jobs and skills**	■ Identifying jobs ■ Identifying job duties	■ Asking and answering questions about jobs ■ Asking and answering questions about job duties	■ Names of jobs ■ Job duties	■ *Yes / No* questions with simple present ■ Short answers with *does* and *doesn't*
Review: Units 7 and 8 pages 108–109		■ Understanding conversations		
Unit 9 **Daily living** pages 110–121 Topic: **Home responsibilities**	■ Identifying family chores	■ Asking and answering questions about family chores ■ Asking and answering questions about people's activities	■ Chores ■ Rooms of a house	■ *What* questions with the present continuous
Unit 10 **Free time** pages 122–133 Topic: **Free-time activities**	■ Identifying free-time activities ■ Describe what people like to do	■ Asking and answering questions about free-time activities	■ Free-time activities	■ *like to* + verb ■ *What* questions with *like to* + verb
Review: Units 9 and 10 pages 134–135		■ Understanding conversations		

READING	WRITING	LIFE SKILLS	PRONUNCIATION
■ Reading a paragraph about a person's schedule ■ Reading someone's daily schedule	■ Completing a schedule ■ Completing sentences about a schedule	■ Reading an invitation	■ Pronouncing key vocabulary ■ Pronouncing times
			■ Pronouncing *a* as in *at* and *o* as in *on*
■ Reading an e-mail about a shopping trip	■ Completing a shopping list	■ Reading a store receipt	■ Pronouncing key vocabulary ■ Pronouncing prices
■ Reading an article about the employee of the month ■ Reading a letter about people's jobs	■ Completing sentences about people's jobs	■ Reading help-wanted ads	■ Pronouncing key vocabulary
			■ Pronouncing *e* as in *red*, *i* as in *six*, and *u* as in *bus*
■ Reading an e-mail about problems with family chores ■ Reading a chart of family chores	■ Completing a chart about family chores ■ Completing sentences about family chores	■ Reading a work order	■ Pronouncing key vocabulary
■ Reading an e-mail to a friend	■ Completing sentences about free-time activities	■ Reading a course description	■ Pronouncing key vocabulary
			■ Reviewing pronunciation of *a*, *e*, *i*, *o*, and *u* in key vocabulary

To the teacher

What is *Ventures*?

Ventures is a six-level, four-skills, standards-based, integrated-skills series that empowers students to achieve their academic and career goals.

- This most complete program with a wealth of resources provides instructors with the tools for any teaching situation.
- The new Online Workbook keeps students learning outside the classroom.
- Easy-to-teach materials make for a more productive classroom.

What components does *Ventures* have?

Student's Book with Audio CD

Each of the core **Student's Books** contains ten topic-focused units, interspersed with five review units. The main units feature six skill-focused lessons.

- **Lessons** in the Student's Book are self-contained, allowing for completion within a one-hour class period.
- **Review lessons** recycle and reinforce the listening, vocabulary, and grammar skills developed in the two prior units and include a pronunciation activity.
- **Self-assessments** in the back of the book give students an opportunity to reflect on their learning. They support learner persistence and help determine whether students are ready for the unit test.
- **Reference charts**, also in the back of the book, provide grammar paradigms; rules for spelling, punctuation, and grammar; and lists of ordinal numbers, cardinal numbers, countries, and nationalities.
- References to the **Self-study audio CD** that accompanies the Student's Book are indicated in the Student's Book by an icon and track number: Look for the audio icon and track number to find activities with self-study audio. "STUDENT" refers to the self-study audio, and "CLASS" refers to the class audio. A full class audio is available separately.
  STUDENT TK 10
  CLASS CD1 TK 14
- A **Student Arcade,** available online at www.cambridge.org/venturesarcade, allows students to practice their skills with interactive activities and download self-study audio.

Teacher's Edition with Assessment Audio CD / CD-ROM

The interleaved **Teacher's Edition** includes easy-to-follow lesson plans for every unit.

- Tips and suggestions address common areas of difficulty for students and provide suggestions for expansion activities and improving learner persistence.

- A **More Ventures** chart at the end of each lesson indicates where to find additional practice material in other *Ventures* components such as the Workbook, Online Teacher's Resource Room (see below), and Student Arcade.
- Unit, midterm, and final tests, which include listening, vocabulary, grammar, reading, and writing sections, are found in the back of the Teacher's Edition.
- The **Assessment Audio CD / CD-ROM** that accompanies the Teacher's Edition contains the audio for each unit, midterm, and final test. It also features all the tests in customizable format so teachers can customize them to suit their needs.

Online Teacher's Resource Room (www.cambridge.org/myresourceroom)

Ventures 2nd Edition offers a free Online Teacher's Resource Room where teachers can download hundreds of additional worksheets and classroom materials including:

- A *placement test* that helps place students into appropriate levels of *Ventures*.
- A *Career and Educational Pathways* solution that helps students identify their educational and career goals.
- *Collaborative activities* for each lesson in Levels 1–4 that develop cooperative learning and community building within the classroom.
- *Writing worksheets* that help Literacy-level students recognize and write shapes, letters, and numbers, while alphabet and number cards promote partner and group work.
- *Picture dictionary cards and worksheets* that reinforce vocabulary learned in Levels Basic, 1, and 2.
- *Extended readings and worksheets* that provide added reading skills development for Levels 3 and 4.
- **Add Ventures** worksheets that were designed for use in multilevel classrooms and in leveled classes where the proficiency level of students differs.

Log on to www.cambridge.org/myresourceroom to explore these and hundreds of other free resources.

Workbook with Audio CD

The **Workbook** provides two pages of activities for each lesson in the Student's Book and includes an audio CD.

- If used in class, the Workbook can extend classroom instructional time by 30 minutes per lesson.
- The exercises are designed so learners can complete them in class or independently. Students can check

their answers with the answer key in the back of the Workbook. Workbook exercises can be assigned in class, for homework, or as student support when a class is missed.

- Grammar charts at the back of the Workbook allow students to use the Workbook for self-study.

Literacy Workbook

The **Literacy Workbook** develops reading and writing readiness skills by focusing on letter formation, the conventions of writing in English, and the connection between written and spoken language. For each lesson in the Basic Student's Book, the Literacy Workbook has two pages of activities focusing on key words and sentences.

- The left-hand page is for students who are pre-, non-, or semiliterate in their own languages.
- The right-hand page is for students who are literate in their first languages, but unfamiliar with the Roman alphabet used in English. When appropriate, students who complete the left-hand page with confidence can move to the right-hand page.
- Students who begin with the right-hand page, but require remediation, can move to the left.

Online Workbooks

The self-grading **Online Workbooks** offer programs the flexibility of introducing blended learning.

- They provide the same high-quality practice opportunities as the print Workbooks and give students instant feedback.
- They allow teachers and programs to track student progress and time on task.

Unit organization

Each unit has six skill-focused lessons:

LESSON A Listening focuses students on the unit topic. The initial exercise, *Before you listen*, creates student interest with visuals that help the teacher assess what learners already know and serve as a prompt for the unit's key vocabulary. Next is *Listen*, which is based on conversations. Students relate vocabulary to meaning and relate the spoken and written forms of new theme-related vocabulary. *After you listen* concludes the lesson by practicing language related to the theme in a communicative activity, either orally with a partner or individually in a writing activity.

LESSONS B AND C focus on grammar. The lessons move from a *Grammar focus* that presents the grammar point in chart form; to *Practice* exercises that check comprehension of the grammar point and provide guided practice; and, finally, to *Communicate* exercises that guide learners as they generate original answers and conversations. These lessons often include a *Culture note*, which provides information directly related to the conversation practice (such as the use of titles with last names), or a *Useful language* note, which introduces useful expressions and functional language.

LESSON D Reading develops reading skills and expands vocabulary. The lesson opens with a *Before you read* exercise, designed to activate prior knowledge and encourage learners to make predictions. A *Reading tip*, which focuses on a specific reading skill, accompanies the *Read* exercise. The reading section of the lesson concludes with *After you read* exercises that check comprehension. In Levels Basic, 1, and 2, the vocabulary expansion portion of the lesson is a *Picture dictionary*. It includes a *word bank*, pictures to identify, and a conversation for practicing the new words. The words expand vocabulary related to the unit topic. In Books 3 and 4, the vocabulary expansion portion of the lesson uses new vocabulary from the reading to build skills such as recognizing word families, selecting definitions based on the context of the reading, and using clues in the reading to guess meaning.

LESSON E Writing provides practice with process writing within the context of the unit. *Before you write* exercises provide warm-up activities to activate the language needed for the writing assignment, followed by one or more exercises that provide a model for students to follow when they write. A *Writing tip* presents information about punctuation or paragraph organization directly related to the writing assignment. The *Write* exercise sets goals for the student writing. In the *After you write* exercise, students share with a partner.

LESSON F Another view has three sections. *Life-skills reading* develops the scanning and skimming skills used with documents such as forms, charts, schedules, announcements, and ads. Multiple-choice questions (modeled on CASAS[1] and BEST[2]) develop test-taking skills. *Fun with vocabulary* provides interactive activities that review and expand the vocabulary of the unit. Finally, *Wrap up* refers students to the self-assessment page in the back of the book, where they can check their knowledge and evaluate their progress.

---

[1] The Comprehensive Adult Student Assessment System. For more information, see www.casas.org.
[2] The Basic English Skills Test. For more information, see www.cal.org/BEST.

Unit tour

The Most Complete Course for Student Success

Ventures empowers students to achieve their academic and career goals.

- The most complete program with a wealth of resources provides instructors with the tools for any teaching situation.
- The new Online Workbook keeps students learning outside the classroom.
- Easy-to-teach materials make for a more productive classroom.

The Big Picture

- Introduces the unit topic and provides rich opportunities for classroom discussion.
- Activates students' prior knowledge and previews the unit vocabulary.

Unit Goals

- Explicit unit goals ensure student involvement in the learning process.

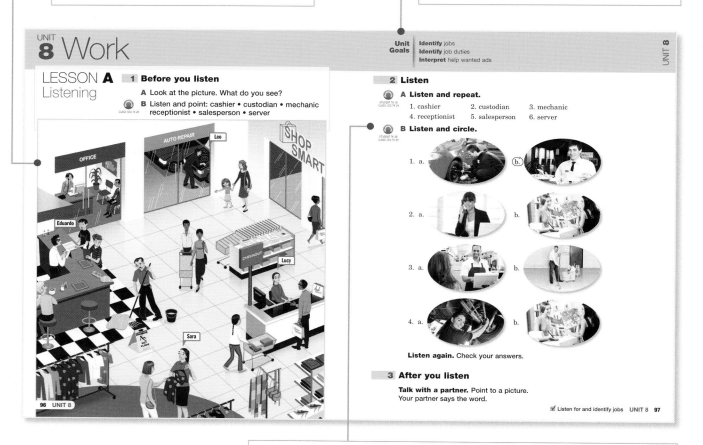

Two Different Audio Programs

- Class audio features over two hours of listening practice to improve listening comprehension.
- Self-study audio encourages learner persistence and autonomy.
- Easy navigation between the two with clear track listings.

Vocabulary Practice

- Explicit vocabulary practice with accompanying audio equips students with the tools necessary to succeed outside the classroom.

Natural Progression

- Students gain fluency and confidence by moving from guided practice to communicative activities.

Real-life Practice

- Meaningful application of the grammar allows for better student engagement.

Grammar Chart

- Clear grammar charts with additional grammar reference in the back of the book allow for greater teacher flexibility.

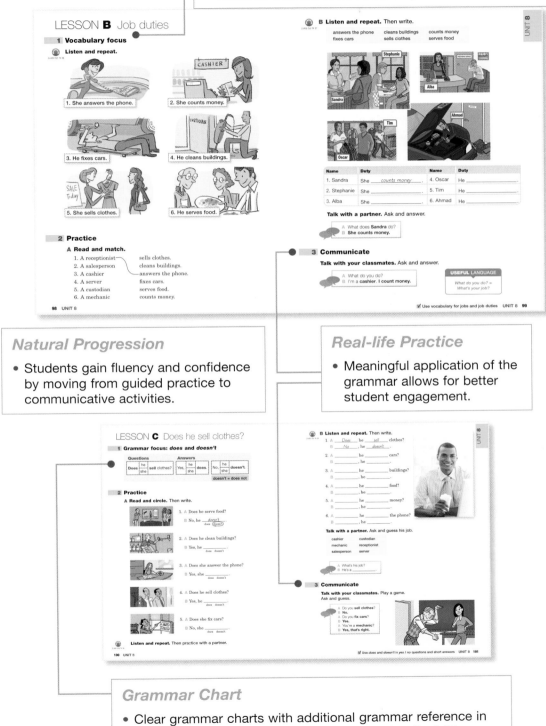

Reading

- *Ventures* features a three-step reading approach that highlights reading strategies and skills needed for success: **Before you read**, **Read**, **After you read**.

Integrated-skills Approach

- Reading is combined with writing and listening for an integrated approach that ensures better comprehension.

Picture Dictionary

- This visual page expands unit vocabulary and works on pronunciation for richer understanding of the topic.

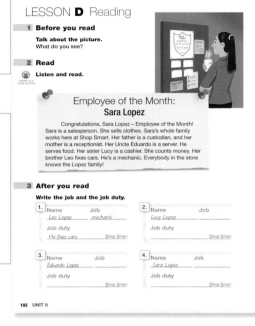

Process Writing

- *Ventures* includes a robust process-writing approach: prewriting, writing, and peer review.

Talk with a Partner

- Spoken practice helps students internalize the vocabulary and relate it to their lives.

Writing for Success

- *Ventures* writing lessons are academic and purposeful, which moves students toward work and educational goals.

Document Literacy

- Explicit practice with authentic-type documents builds real-life skills.

Fun with Vocabulary

- Interactive activities provide review and expand the vocabulary of the unit.

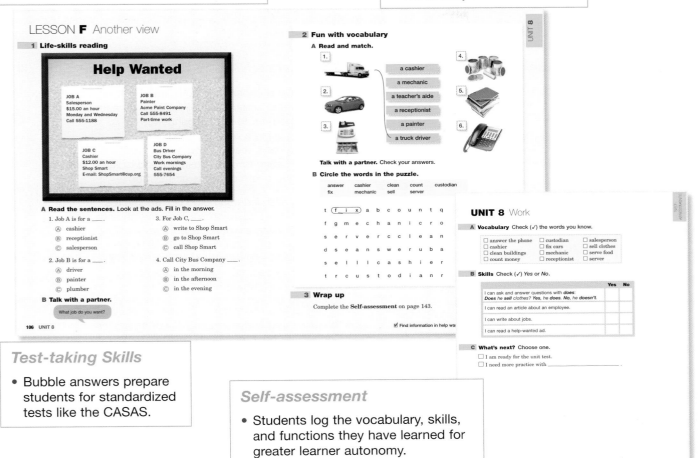

Test-taking Skills

- Bubble answers prepare students for standardized tests like the CASAS.

Self-assessment

- Students log the vocabulary, skills, and functions they have learned for greater learner autonomy.

Review

- An integrated-skills approach reinforces the language of the previous two units.

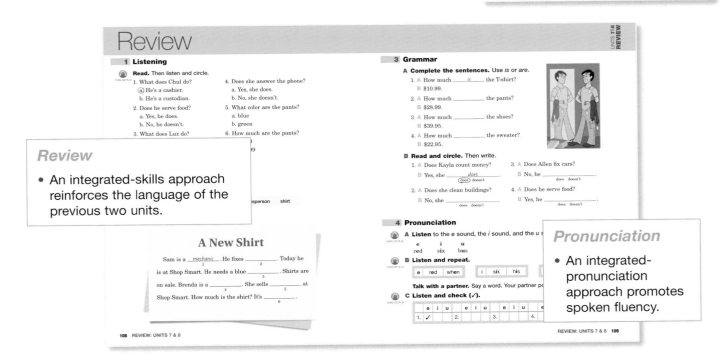

Pronunciation

- An integrated-pronunciation approach promotes spoken fluency.

Correlations

UNIT	CASAS Competencies	NRS Educational Functioning Level Descriptors Oral BEST: 0–15 (SPL 0–1) BEST Plus: 400 and below (SPL 0–1) BEST Literacy: 0–7 (SPL 0–1)
Unit 1 **Personal information** Pages 6–17	0.1.2, 0.1.4, 0.1.5, 0.2.1, 2.3.2, 4.8.1, 6.0.1, 7.4.1, 7.4.2, 7.4.3, 7.5.1	▪ Speaking and understanding isolated words ▪ Speaking and understanding isolated phrases ▪ Connecting print to spoken language ▪ Practicing using a writing instrument ▪ Practicing basic reading and writing skills ▪ Communicating through gestures and isolated words ▪ Recognizing common signs and symbols
Unit 2 **At school** Pages 18–29	0.1.2, 0.1.5, 1.4.1, 2.3.2, 4.5.1, 4.8.1, 7.4.1, 7.4.2, 7.4.3, 7.5.1	▪ Speaking and understanding isolated words ▪ Speaking and understanding isolated phrases ▪ Practicing using a writing instrument ▪ Practicing basic reading and writing skills ▪ Communicating through gestures and isolated words ▪ Recognizing common signs and symbols ▪ Exposure to computers or technology
Unit 3 **Friends and family** Pages 32–43	0.1.2, 0.1.4, 0.1.5, 0.2.1, 4.8.1, 7.4.1, 7.4.2, 7.4.3, 7.5.1, 8.3.1	▪ Speaking and understanding isolated words ▪ Speaking and understanding isolated phrases ▪ Connecting print to spoken language ▪ Practicing using a writing instrument ▪ Practicing basic reading and writing skills ▪ Communicating through gestures and isolated words ▪ Exposure to computers or technology
Unit 4 **Health** Pages 44–55	0.1.2, 0.1.4, 0.1.5, 0.2.1, 3.1.1, 3.1.3, 3.3.1, 3.3.2, 3.4.1, 4.8.1, 7.4.1, 7.4.2, 7.4.3, 7.5.1, 8.3.2	▪ Speaking and understanding isolated words ▪ Speaking and understanding isolated phrases ▪ Connecting print to spoken language ▪ Practicing using a writing instrument ▪ Practicing basic reading and writing skills ▪ Communicating through gestures and isolated words ▪ Recognizing common signs and symbols
Unit 5 **Around town** Pages 58–69	0.1.2, 0.1.4, 0.1.5, 0.2.1, 1.1.3, 2.2.1, 2.2.3, 2.2.5, 2.5.4, 4.8.1, 7.1.1, 7.4.1, 7.4.2, 7.4.3, 7.4.8, 7.5.1, 7.5.6	▪ Speaking and understanding isolated words ▪ Speaking and understanding isolated phrases ▪ Connecting print to spoken language ▪ Practicing using a writing instrument ▪ Practicing basic reading and writing skills ▪ Communicating through gestures and isolated words ▪ Recognizing common signs and symbols

All units of *Ventures 2nd Edition* meet most of the EFF content standards and provide overall BEST test preparation. The chart above lists areas of particular focus.

For more details and correlations to other state standards, go to: www.cambridge.org/myresourceroom

EFF	Florida Adult ESOL	LAUSD ESL Beginning Literacy Competencies
▪ Conveying ideas in writing ▪ Cooperating with others ▪ Listening actively ▪ Reading with understanding ▪ Reflecting and evaluating ▪ Speaking so others can understand ▪ Taking responsibility for learning	1.01.01, 1.01.02, 1.01.03, 1.01.04, 1.01.05, 1.01.06, 1.01.10, 1.03.12, 1.04.01	I. 1a, 1b, 1c, 2, 3, 4 II. 5m III. 8, 9
▪ Assessing what one knows already ▪ Organizing and presenting information ▪ Paying attention to the conventions of spoken English ▪ Seeking feedback and revising accordingly ▪ Working with pictures and numbers ▪ Cooperating with others ▪ Speaking so others can understand	1.01.02, 1.01.04, 1.01.05, 1.03.10, 1.03.12, 1.03.16, 1.04.09	I. 3 II. 6b III. 8, 9, 11
▪ Conveying ideas in writing ▪ Cooperating with others ▪ Listening actively ▪ Monitoring comprehension and adjusting reading strategies ▪ Offering clear input on own interests and attitudes ▪ Organizing and presenting information ▪ Speaking so others can understand	1.01.03, 1.02.07, 1.03.12, 1.04.04, 1.05.01	I. 1d, 3 III. 9
▪ Anticipating and identifying problems ▪ Attending to oral information ▪ Interacting with others in ways that are friendly, courteous, and tactful ▪ Solving problems and making decisions ▪ Speaking so others can understand ▪ Using strategies appropriate to goals ▪ Cooperating with others	1.01.04, 1.02.07, 1.03.12, 1.03.16, 1.05.01, 1.05.02, 1.05.03, 1.05.04, 1.07.03	I. 3 II. 7 III. 9
▪ Seeking feedback and revising accordingly ▪ Seeking input from others ▪ Selecting appropriate reading strategies ▪ Speaking so others can understand ▪ Taking responsibility for learning ▪ Cooperating with others	1.01.03, 1.02.01, 1.02.02, 1.02.10, 1.03.12, 1.04.09, 1.06.01, 1.06.02, 1.06.03	I. 3 II. 5k III. 10

UNIT	CASAS Competencies	NRS Educational Functioning Level Descriptors *Oral BEST: 0–15 (SPL 0–1)* *BEST Plus: 400 and below (SPL 0–1)* *BEST Literacy: 0–7 (SPL 0–1)*
Unit 6 **Time** Pages 70–81	0.1.2, 0.1.4, 0.1.5, 0.2.1, 2.3.1, 2.3.2, 4.5.3, 4.8.1, 6.0.1, 7.1.1, 7.1.4, 7.4.1, 7.4.2, 7.4.3, 7.5.1	▪ Speaking and understanding isolated words ▪ Speaking and understanding isolated phrases ▪ Connecting print to spoken language ▪ Practicing using a writing instrument ▪ Practicing basic reading and writing skills ▪ Communicating through gestures and isolated words ▪ Recognizing common signs and symbols
Unit 7 **Shopping** Pages 84–95	0.1.2, 0.1.4, 0.1.5, 0.2.1, 1.1.6, 1.2.1, 1.2.2, 1.3.9, 1.6.3, 4.8.1, 6.0.1, 7.1.1, 7.4.1, 7.4.2, 7.4.3, 7.5.1, 8.1.4	▪ Speaking and understanding isolated words ▪ Speaking and understanding isolated phrases ▪ Connecting print to spoken language ▪ Practicing using a writing instrument ▪ Practicing basic reading and writing skills ▪ Communicating through gestures and isolated words ▪ Exposure to computers or technology
Unit 8 **Work** Pages 96–107	0.1.2, 0.1.4, 0.1.5, 0.2.1, 1.1.6, 2.3.2, 4.1.3, 4.1.6, 4.1.8, 4.8.1, 4.8.2, 6.0.1, 7.1.1, 7.1.4, 7.4.1, 7.4.2, 7.5.1	▪ Speaking and understanding isolated words ▪ Speaking and understanding isolated phrases ▪ Practicing using a writing instrument ▪ Practicing basic reading and writing skills ▪ Communicating name and other personal information ▪ Practicing entry-level job-related writing ▪ Practicing entry-level job-related speaking
Unit 9 **Daily living** Pages 110–121	0.1.2, 0.1.5, 0.2.1, 0.2.4, 1.4.1, 1.7.4, 4.1.8, 4.7.3, 4.7.4, 4.8.1, 7.1.1, 7.4.1, 7.4.2, 7.4.3, 7.5.6, 8.1.4, 8.2.1, 8.2.2, 8.2.3, 8.2.4, 8.2.5	▪ Speaking and understanding isolated words ▪ Speaking and understanding isolated phrases ▪ Connecting print to spoken language ▪ Practicing using a writing instrument ▪ Practicing basic reading and writing skills ▪ Recognizing common signs and symbols ▪ Exposure to computers or technology
Unit 10 **Free time** Pages 122–133	0.1.1, 0.1.2, 0.1.4, 0.1.5, 0.2.1, 0.2.4, 2.3.1, 2.3.2, 4.8.1, 7.1.1, 7.4.1, 7.4.2, 7.4.3, 7.5.1, 7.5.6	▪ Speaking and understanding isolated words ▪ Connecting print to spoken language ▪ Practicing using a writing instrument ▪ Practicing basic reading and writing skills ▪ Communicating through gestures and isolated words ▪ Recognizing common signs and symbols ▪ Exposure to computers or technology

All units of *Ventures 2nd Edition* meet most of the EFF content standards and provide overall BEST test preparation. The chart above lists areas of particular focus.

For more details and correlations to other state standards, go to: www.cambridge.org/myresourceroom

EFF	Florida Adult ESOL	LAUSD ESL Beginning Literacy Competencies
▪ Attending to oral information ▪ Identifying own strengths and weaknesses as a learner ▪ Interacting with others in ways that are friendly, courteous, and tactful ▪ Monitoring comprehension and adjusting reading strategies ▪ Organizing and presenting information ▪ Cooperating with others ▪ Speaking so others can understand	1.01.03, 1.01.05, 1.02.02, 1.03.09, 1.03.12, 1.03.16, 1.04.01	I. 3 II. 6a, 6c
▪ Cooperating with others ▪ Listening actively ▪ Reading with understanding ▪ Reflecting and evaluating ▪ Speaking so others can understand ▪ Taking responsibility for learning	1.01.03, 1.03.12, 1.03.16, 1.04.01, 1.04.02, 1.04.06	I. 3 III. 13, 14
▪ Attending to oral information ▪ Listening actively ▪ Monitoring comprehension and adjusting reading strategies ▪ Reading with understanding ▪ Reflecting and evaluating ▪ Speaking so others can understand ▪ Cooperating with others	1.01.03, 1.03.01, 1.03.02, 1.03.12, 1.03.14	I. 3 III. 8, 13
▪ Identifying own strengths and weaknesses as a learner ▪ Interacting with others in ways that are friendly, courteous, and tactful ▪ Monitoring progress toward goals ▪ Offering clear input on own interests and attitudes ▪ Organizing and presenting information ▪ Reading with understanding ▪ Cooperating with others ▪ Speaking so others can understand	1.01.03, 1.01.04, 1.03.12	I. 3 II. 7 III. 8
▪ Conveying ideas in writing ▪ Cooperating with others ▪ Listening actively ▪ Reading with understanding ▪ Reflecting and evaluating ▪ Speaking so others can understand ▪ Taking responsibility for learning	1.01.02, 1.01.03, 1.01.04, 1.03.12	I. 3 II. 5

Meet the *Ventures* author team

Gretchen Bitterlin has been an ESL teacher and an ESL department chair. She is currently the ESL coordinator for the Continuing Education Program at San Diego Community College District. Under Gretchen's leadership, the ESL program has developed several products – for example, an ESL oral interview placement test and writing rubrics for assessing writing for level exit – now used by other agencies. She is a co-author of *English for Adult Competency*, has been an item writer for CASAS tests, and chaired the task force that developed the TESOL *Adult Education Program Standards*. She is a recipient of her district's award, Outstanding Contract Faculty. Gretchen holds an MA in TESOL from the University of Arizona.

Dennis Johnson had his first language-teaching experience as a Peace Corps volunteer in South Korea. Following that teaching experience, he became an in-country ESL trainer. After returning to the United States, he became an ESL trainer and began teaching credit and non-credit ESL at City College of San Francisco. As ESL site coordinator, he has provided guidance to faculty in selecting textbooks. He is the author of *Get Up and Go* and co-author of *The Immigrant Experience*. Dennis is the demonstration teacher on the *Ventures Professional Development DVD*. Dennis holds an MA in music from Stanford University.

Donna Price began her ESL career teaching EFL in Madagascar. She is currently associate professor of ESL and vocational ESL / technology resource instructor for the Continuing Education Program, San Diego Community College District. She has served as an author and a trainer for CALPRO, the California Adult Literacy Professional Development Project, co-authoring training modules on contextualizing and integrating workforce skills into the ESL classroom. She is a recipient of the TESOL Newbury House Award for Excellence in Teaching, and she is author of *Skills for Success*. Donna holds an MA in linguistics from San Diego State University.

Sylvia Ramirez started as an instructional aide in ESL. Since then she has been a part-time teacher, a full-time teacher, and a program coordinator. As program coordinator at Mira Costa College, she provided leadership in establishing Managed Enrollment, Student Learning Outcomes, and Transitioning Adults to Academic and Career Preparation. Her more than forty years in adult ESL includes multilevel ESL, vocational ESL, family literacy, and distance learning. She has also provided technical assistance to local ESL programs for the California State Department of Education. In 2011 she received the Hayward Award in education. Her MA is in education / counseling from Point Loma University, and she has certificates in TESOL and in online teaching.

K. Lynn Savage first taught English in Japan. She began teaching ESL at City College of San Francisco in 1974, where she has taught all levels of non-credit ESL and has served as vocational ESL resource teacher. She has trained teachers for adult education programs around the country as well as abroad. She chaired the committee that developed *ESL Model Standards for Adult Education Programs* (California, 1992) and is the author, co-author, and editor of many ESL materials including *Crossroads Café, Teacher Training through Video, Parenting for Academic Success, Building Life Skills, Picture Stories, May I Help You?,* and *English That Works*. Lynn holds an MA in TESOL from Teachers College, Columbia University.

To the student

Welcome to **Ventures** *Basic*!

Enjoy your book in class.

Enjoy your book at home.

Your book has an audio CD in the back. Look for the picture 🎧 in your book. Then listen to the CD, and review and practice at home.

Good luck!

The Author Team
Gretchen Bitterlin
Dennis Johnson
Donna Price
Sylvia Ramirez
K. Lynn Savage

Welcome

1 Meet your classmates

Look at the picture. What do you see?

2 The alphabet

A Listen and point. Look at the alphabet.

STUDENT TK 2
CLASS CD1 TK 2

Aa	Bb	Cc	Dd	Ee	Ff	Gg	Hh	Ii
Jj	Kk	Ll	Mm	Nn	Oo	Pp	Qq	Rr
Ss	Tt	Uu	Vv	Ww	Xx	Yy	Zz	

Listen again and repeat.

B Listen and write.

STUDENT TK 3
CLASS CD1 TK 3

1. _A_ nita   2. ____ aniel   3. ____ eizhi   4. ____ uri
5. ____ ranco   6. ____ ee   7. ____ akim   8. ____ arla

C Write your name.

_____

Talk with 3 classmates. Say your name. Spell your name.

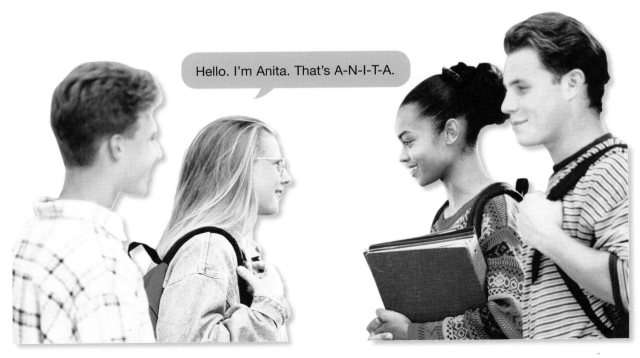

Hello. I'm Anita. That's A-N-I-T-A.

3 Classroom directions

A Listen and point. Look at the pictures.

STUDENT TK 4
CLASS CD1 TK 4

1. Look.

2. Listen.

3. Point.

4. Repeat.

Book.
Book.

5. Talk.

6. Write.

7. Read.

8. Circle.
book
Pencil

9. Match.
book
pencil

Listen again and repeat.

B Talk with a partner. Say a word.
Your partner points to the picture.

Look.

4 Numbers

STUDENT TK 5
CLASS CD1 TK 5

A Listen and point. Look at the numbers.

1 one	2 two	3 three	4 four	5 five
6 six	7 seven	8 eight	9 nine	10 ten
11 eleven	12 twelve	13 thirteen	14 fourteen	15 fifteen
16 sixteen	17 seventeen	18 eighteen	19 nineteen	20 twenty

Listen again and repeat.

STUDENT TK 6
CLASS CD1 TK 6

B Listen and write the number.

1. _____6_____   2. _____   3. _____   4. _____

5. _____   6. _____   7. _____   8. _____

Talk with a partner. Check your answers.

LESSON **A**
Listening

1 **Before you listen**

A Look at the picture. What do you see?

CLASS CD1 TK 7

B Listen and point: area code • country • first name
ID card • last name • phone number

2 Listen

A Listen and repeat.

STUDENT TK 7
CLASS CD1 TK 8

1. area code
2. country
3. first name
4. ID card
5. last name
6. phone number

B Listen and circle.

STUDENT TK 8
CLASS CD1 TK 9

1. a.    b.

2. a.    b.

3. a.    b.

4. a.    b.

Listen again. Check your answers.

3 After you listen

Talk with a partner. Point to a picture.
Your partner says the words.

☑ Listen for and identify personal information   **UNIT 1**   **7**

LESSON **B** Countries

1 Vocabulary focus

🎧 **Listen and repeat.**

CLASS CD1 TK 10

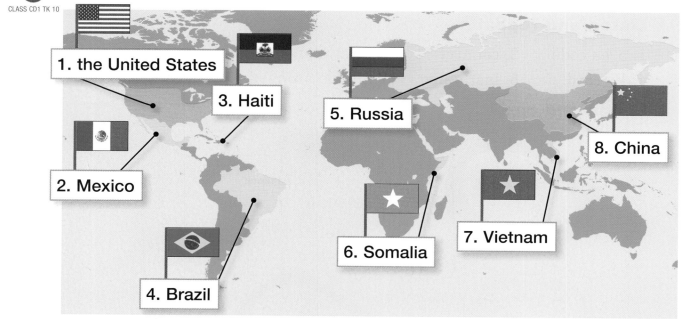

1. the United States
2. Mexico
3. Haiti
4. Brazil
5. Russia
6. Somalia
7. Vietnam
8. China

2 Practice

A Read and match.

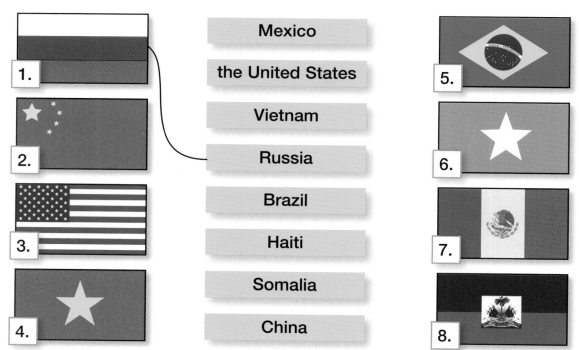

Mexico

the United States

Vietnam

Russia

Brazil

Haiti

Somalia

China

B Listen and repeat. Then write.

CLASS CD1 TK 11

Name	Country	Name	Country
1. Ivan	*Russia*	4. Elsa	
2. Asad		5. Luisa	
3. Eduardo		6. Jun-Ming	

Talk with a partner. Ask and answer.

> A Where is **Ivan** from?
> B **Russia.**

3 Communicate

Talk in a group. Ask and answer. Complete the chart.

> A What's your name?
> B **Binh.**
> A Where are you from?
> B **Vietnam.**

Name	Country
Binh	*Vietnam*

☑ Name countries of origin **UNIT 1** **9**

LESSON C What's your name?

1 Grammar focus: *my, your, his, her*

Questions			Answers		
What's	your	name?	My	name is	Angela.
	his		His		Kevin.
	her		Her		Julia.

What's = What is

2 Practice

A Read and circle. Then write.

1. **A** What's your name?
   B ___*My*___ name is Nancy.
   (My) Your

2. **A** What's his name?
   B _____ name is Chin.
   His   Her

3. **A** What's her name?
   B _____ name is Alima.
   His   Her

4. **A** What's your name?
   B _____ name is Vincent.
   My   Your

Listen and repeat. Then practice with a partner.

CLASS CD1 TK 13

B Listen and repeat. Then write.

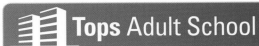 Tops Adult School

First name: Jack
Last name: Lee
Area code: 203
Phone number: 555-9687

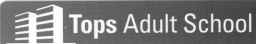 Tops Adult School

First name: Sara
Last name: Garza
Area code: 415
Phone number: 555-3702

What's his . . . ?		What's her . . . ?	
1. first _name_	Jack	5. _____ code	415
2. last _____	Lee	6. _____ number	555-3702
3. area _____	203	7. _____ name	Garza
4. phone _____	555-9687	8. _____ name	Sara

Talk with a partner. Ask and answer.

A What's **his first name**?
B **Jack.**

3 Communicate

Talk with your classmates. Complete the chart.

A What's your **first name**?
B My **first name** is **Yuri**.

USEFUL LANGUAGE

How do you spell Yuri?
Y-U-R-I

First name	Last name	Area code	Phone number
Yuri			

☑ Use *my, your, his,* and *her* to ask and answer questions about names   **UNIT 1**   **11**

LESSON **D** Reading

1 Before you read

Talk about the picture.
What do you see?

2 Read

 Listen and read.

STUDENT TK 9
CLASS CD1 TK 14

Welcome!

Meet our new student.

His first name is Ernesto.

His last name is Delgado.

He is from Mexico.

Welcome, Ernesto Delgado!

3 After you read

Read the sentences. Circle *Yes* or *No*.

1. His name is Ernesto Mexico.   Yes   (No)
2. His first name is Ernesto.   Yes   No
3. His last name is Delgado.   Yes   No
4. He is from Ecuador.   Yes   No

4 Picture dictionary Months of the year

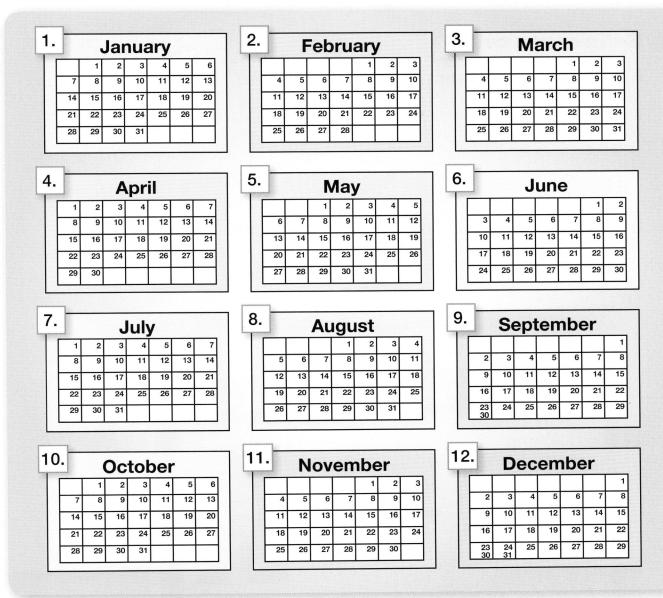

1. **January**

	1	2	3	4	5	6
7	8	9	10	11	12	13
14	15	16	17	18	19	20
21	22	23	24	25	26	27
28	29	30	31			

2. **February**

				1	2	3
4	5	6	7	8	9	10
11	12	13	14	15	16	17
18	19	20	21	22	23	24
25	26	27	28			

3. **March**

				1	2	3
4	5	6	7	8	9	10
11	12	13	14	15	16	17
18	19	20	21	22	23	24
25	26	27	28	29	30	31

4. **April**

1	2	3	4	5	6	7
8	9	10	11	12	13	14
15	16	17	18	19	20	21
22	23	24	25	26	27	28
29	30					

5. **May**

	1	2	3	4	5
6	7	8	9	10	11	12
13	14	15	16	17	18	19
20	21	22	23	24	25	26
27	28	29	30	31		

6. **June**

					1	2
3	4	5	6	7	8	9
10	11	12	13	14	15	16
17	18	19	20	21	22	23
24	25	26	27	28	29	30

7. **July**

1	2	3	4	5	6	7
8	9	10	11	12	13	14
15	16	17	18	19	20	21
22	23	24	25	26	27	28
29	30	31				

8. **August**

			1	2	3	4
5	6	7	8	9	10	11
12	13	14	15	16	17	18
19	20	21	22	23	24	25
26	27	28	29	30	31	

9. **September**

						1
2	3	4	5	6	7	8
9	10	11	12	13	14	15
16	17	18	19	20	21	22
23 30	24	25	26	27	28	29

10. **October**

	1	2	3	4	5	6
7	8	9	10	11	12	13
14	15	16	17	18	19	20
21	22	23	24	25	26	27
28	29	30	31			

11. **November**

				1	2	3
4	5	6	7	8	9	10
11	12	13	14	15	16	17
18	19	20	21	22	23	24
25	26	27	28	29	30	

12. **December**

						1
2	3	4	5	6	7	8
9	10	11	12	13	14	15
16	17	18	19	20	21	22
23 30	24 31	25	26	27	28	29

A Listen and repeat. Look at the picture dictionary.

STUDENT TK 10
CLASS CD1 TK 15

B Talk with your classmates. Complete the chart.

A What's your name?
B **Eva.**
A When's your birthday?
B **In April.**

Name	Month
Eva	*April*

LESSON E Writing

1 Before you write

A Talk with a partner. Complete the words.

1. _f_ i r s t
2. ___ a s t
3. ___ a m e
4. a r e a ___ o d e
5. p h o n e ___ u m b e r

B Read the ID card. Complete the sentences.

Central Adult School Library

Wong
Last name

Linda
First name

916
Area code

555-7834
Phone number

China
Country

Linda Wong
Signature

CULTURE NOTE

Your signature is how you write your name.

1. Her _____ _____ is Linda.
2. Her _____ _____ is Wong.
3. Her _____ _____ is 916.
4. Her _____ _____ is 555-7834.
5. She is from _____.

2 Write

A Complete the ID card. Write about yourself.

Central Adult School Library

_____
Last name

_____
First name

_____
Area code

_____
Phone number

_____
Country

_____
Signature

B Complete the sentences. Write about yourself.

1. My first name is _____.
2. My last name is _____.
3. My area code is _____.
4. My phone number is _____.
5. My birthday is in _____.

3 After you write

Talk with a partner. Share your writing.

LESSON F Another view

A Read the sentences. Look at the ID card. Fill in the answer.

1. His first name is ___.
   - (A) Ahmed
   - (B) Woodrow
   - ● Samir

2. His area code is ___.
   - (A) 33612
   - (B) 813
   - (C) 555

3. His birthday is in ___.
   - (A) January
   - (B) February
   - (C) August

4. His last name is ___.
   - (A) Ahmed
   - (B) Woodrow
   - (C) Tampa

B Talk with a partner.

Say two things about Samir.

2 Fun with vocabulary

A What word is different? Circle the word.

1. Countries

Mexico	China	~~November~~	Somalia

2. Months

April	September	May	Russia

3. Phone numbers

555-4861	555-6978	415	555-7934

4. Area codes

555-6948	813	212	915

5. First names

Linda	Alima	Nasser	Mexico

6. Last names

Cruz	February	Delgado	Lee

Talk with a partner. Check your answers.

B Work with a partner. Write the months in order.

April	August	December	February	January	July
June	March	May		November	October	September

1 January	2	3	4
5	**6**	**7**	**8**
9	**10**	**11**	**12**

3 Wrap up

Complete the **Self-assessment** on page 136.

LESSON A
Listening

1 Before you listen

A Look at the picture. What do you see?

B Listen and point: a book • a chair • a computer a desk • a notebook • a pencil

CLASS CD1 TK 16

2 Listen

A Listen and repeat.

STUDENT TK 11
CLASS CD1 TK 17

1. a book   2. a chair   3. a computer
4. a desk   5. a notebook   6. a pencil

B Listen and circle.

STUDENT TK 12
CLASS CD1 TK 18

1. a.    (b.)

2. a.    b.

3. a.    b.

4. a.    b.

Listen again. Check your answers.

3 After you listen

Talk with a partner. Point to a picture.
Your partner says the word.

LESSON **B** Classroom objects

1 Vocabulary focus

Listen and repeat.

CLASS CD1 TK 19

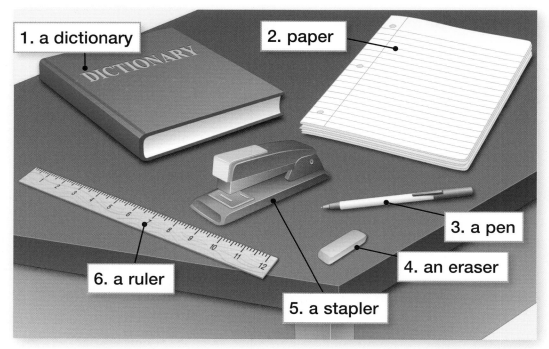

1. a dictionary

2. paper

3. a pen

4. an eraser

5. a stapler

6. a ruler

2 Practice

A Read and match.

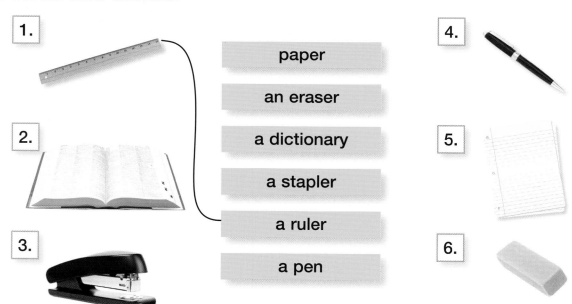

1.

2.

3.

paper

an eraser

a dictionary

a stapler

a ruler

a pen

4.

5.

6.

B Listen and repeat. Then write.

| a dictionary | an eraser | paper |
| a pen | a ruler | a stapler |

1. *a dictionary*
2. _____
3. _____
4. _____
5. _____
6. _____

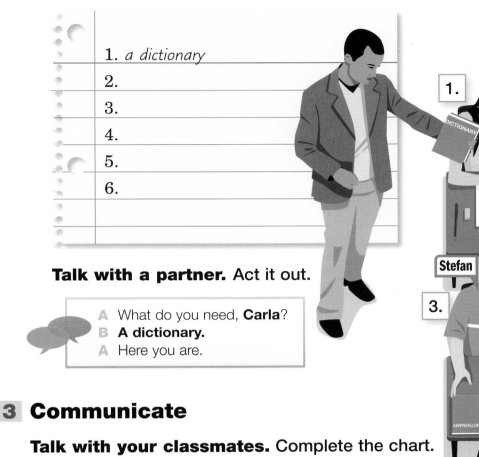

Talk with a partner. Act it out.

A What do you need, **Carla**?
B **A dictionary.**
A Here you are.

3 Communicate

Talk with your classmates. Complete the chart.

A What do you need, **Mahmoud**?
B **An eraser.**

Name	Classroom object
Mahmoud	*an eraser*

LESSON C Where's my pencil?

1 Grammar focus: *in*, *on*, and *under*

in the desk

on the desk

under the desk

2 Practice

A Read and circle. Then write.

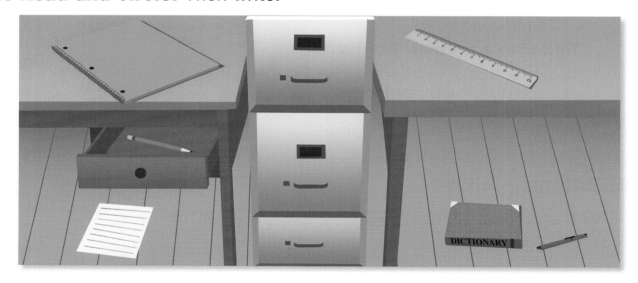

1. A Where's my pencil?

   B _____*In*_____ the desk.
   (In) On Under

2. A Where's my notebook?

   B _____ the desk.
   In On Under

3. A Where's my pen?

   B _____ the floor.
   In On Under

4. A Where's my dictionary?

   B _____ the table.
   In On Under

5. A Where's my ruler?

   B _____ the table.
   In On Under

6. A Where's my paper?

   B _____ the desk.
   In On Under

Listen and repeat. Then practice with a partner.

CLASS CD1 TK 21

B Look at the picture. Match the words.

1. my book — under the chair
2. my stapler — on the desk
3. my notebook — in the desk
4. my ruler — on the book

5. my paper — in the notebook
6. my pen — under the desk
7. my pencil — on the paper
8. my dictionary — on the chair

Talk with a partner. Act it out.

A Where's my **book**?
B **In the desk.**
A Thanks.

3 Communicate

Talk with a partner. Complete the chart.

A Where's my **pencil**?
B **On the desk.**

USEFUL LANGUAGE

I don't know.

my pencil	*on the desk*
my book	
my paper	
my pen	
my dictionary	
my notebook	

LESSON **D** Reading

1 Before you read

Talk about the picture.
What do you see?

2 Read

Listen and read.

STUDENT TK 13
CLASS CD1 TK 22

Sue,

It's Monday, your first day of English class! You need a pencil, eraser, notebook, and dictionary. The pencil is in the desk. The eraser is on the desk. The notebook is on my computer. And the dictionary is under the chair.

Have fun at school!

Mom

3 After you read

Read and match.

1.

The pencil is in
the desk.

The notebook is
on the computer.

3.

The dictionary is
under the chair.

2.

The eraser is on
the desk.

4.

4 **Picture dictionary** Days of the week

MARCH

SUNDAY
2

MONDAY
3

TUESDAY
4

WEDNESDAY
5

THURSDAY
6

FRIDAY
7

SATURDAY
8

STUDENT TK 14
CLASS CD1 TK 23

A **Listen and repeat.** Look at the picture dictionary.

B **Talk with a partner.** Point and ask. Your partner answers.

A What day is it?
B **Monday.**

☑ Read a note about the location of school items; name the days of the week   **UNIT 2**   **25**

LESSON **E** Writing

1 Before you write

A Talk with a partner. Complete the words.

1. e r a s e __r__
2. d i c t i o n a r ___
3. p e ___
4. p e n c i ___
5. n o t e b o o ___

B Talk with a partner. Look at the picture. Write the words.

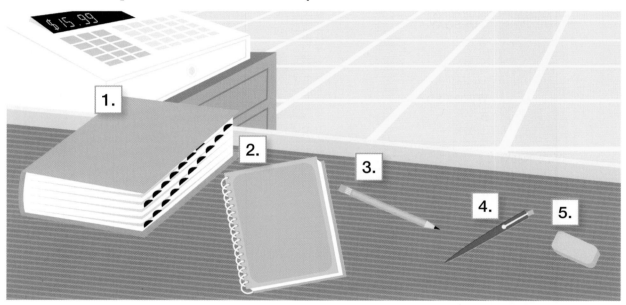

1. *dictionary*
2.
3.
4.
5.

2 Write

A Read the memo.

Welcome to Miami Adult School!

M
AS

The first day of school is Monday.

Your teacher is Ms. Moreno.

Your class is in Room 101.

For class, you need:

    a dictionary

    a notebook

    a pencil

    a pen

    an eraser

B Complete the memo. Write about yourself.

The first day of school is _____.

My teacher is _____.

My class is in Room _____.

For class, I need _____.

I need _____.

I need _____.

I need _____.

I need _____.

3 After you write

Talk with a partner. Share your writing.

LESSON F Another view

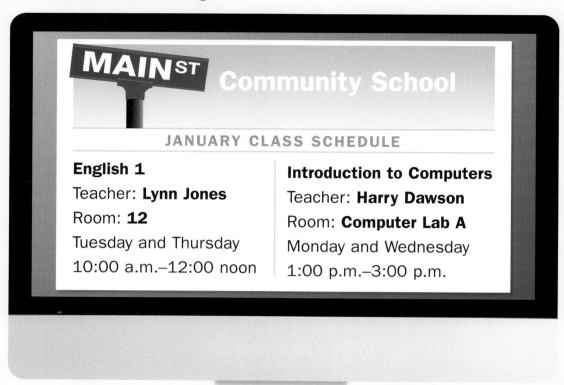

MAINST **Community School**

JANUARY CLASS SCHEDULE

English 1	**Introduction to Computers**
Teacher: **Lynn Jones**	Teacher: **Harry Dawson**
Room: **12**	Room: **Computer Lab A**
Tuesday and Thursday	Monday and Wednesday
10:00 a.m.–12:00 noon	1:00 p.m.–3:00 p.m.

A Read the sentences. Look at the class schedule.
Fill in the answer.

1. The English class is on ____ .
   - Ⓐ Monday and Wednesday
   - Ⓑ Tuesday and Thursday
   - Ⓒ Tuesday and Wednesday

2. The computer class is on ____ .
   - Ⓐ Monday and Wednesday
   - Ⓑ Tuesday and Thursday
   - Ⓒ Monday and Tuesday

3. The English class is in ____ .
   - Ⓐ Room 1
   - Ⓑ Room 12
   - Ⓒ Lab A

4. The computer class is in ____ .
   - Ⓐ Lab A
   - Ⓑ Lab B
   - Ⓒ Room 1

B Talk with a partner.

Talk about your class schedule.

2 Fun with vocabulary

A Talk with a partner. What's in your classroom? Check (✓).

☐ a book   ☐ a chair   ☐ a computer

☐ a desk   ☐ a dictionary   ☐ an eraser

☐ a notebook   ☐ paper   ☐ a pen

☐ a pencil   ☐ a ruler   ☐ a stapler

B Circle the words in the puzzle.

book	chair	computer	desk	dictionary	eraser
notebook	paper	pen	pencil	ruler	stapler

```
h   s   h   f   e  (b   o   o   k)  t   z   a

q   u   p   e   n   c   i   l   a   f   r   s

l   i   g   o   w   n   e   r   a   s   e   r

v   y   b   d   e   s   k   a   f   l   k   o

d   i   c   t   i   o   n   a   r   y   o   j

f   e   t   h   s   t   a   p   l   e   r   e

w   r   n   n   o   t   e   b   o   o   k   r

p   e   n   k   v   l   z   o   j   s   y   n

o   t   c   o   m   p   u   t   e   r   m   q

t   r   u   l   e   r   g   a   r   x   z   a

h   o   m   t   c   z   e   c   h   a   i   r

p   a   p   e   r   n   y   i   d   e   m   t
```

3 Wrap up

Complete the **Self-assessment** on page 137.

Review

1 Listening

CLASS CD1 TK 24

Read. Then listen and circle.

1. What's his first name?
   a. Ali
   b. Hassan
2. What's his last name?
   a. Ali
   b. Garcia
3. Where is he from?
   a. Mexico
   b. Somalia

4. When is his birthday?
   a. in August
   b. in October
5. Where's the notebook?
   a. on the desk
   b. on the chair
6. Where's the paper?
   a. in the notebook
   b. on the chair

Talk with a partner. Ask and answer.

2 Vocabulary

Write. Complete the story.

book   Brazil   card   February   name   Tuesday

Welcome, Luisa Pinto!

Luisa is a new student. She is from ____Brazil____. Her
                                        1

last _____ is Pinto. Her birthday is in _____.
        2   3

In fact, her birthday is on _____. Happy birthday!
                                 4

Luisa needs a _____ and an ID _____.
                  5   6

Welcome, Luisa!

3 Grammar

A Complete the sentences.

Use *in*, *on*, or *under*.

1. The pen is ___under___ the notebook.

2. The dictionary is _____ the desk.

3. The book is _____ the chair.

4. The stapler is _____ the desk.

B Read and circle. Then write.

1. ___His___ name is Alberto.
   (His) Her

2. _____ name is Layla.
   His   Her

3. A What is _____ name?
       his   your

   B _____ name is Kim.
     My   Your

4 Pronunciation

CLASS CD1 TK 25

A Listen to the *a* sound and the *o* sound.

a	o
name	phone

CLASS CD1 TK 26

B Listen and repeat.

a	name	day	say

o	phone	code	note

Talk with a partner. Say a word. Your partner points. Take turns.

CLASS CD1 TK 27

C Listen and check (✓).

	a	o		a	o		a	o		a	o		a	o
1.	✓		2.			3.			4.			5.		

LESSON A
Listening

1 Before you listen

A Look at the picture. What do you see?

 B Listen and point: daughter • father
grandfather • grandmother • mother • son

CLASS CD1 TK 28

Unit Goals	**Identify** family members
	Describe a family picture
	Interpret a housing application

2 Listen

A Listen and repeat.

STUDENT TK 15
CLASS CD1 TK 29

1. daughter   2. father   3. grandfather

4. grandmother   5. mother   6. son

B Listen and circle.

STUDENT TK 16
CLASS CD1 TK 30

1. (a.)    b.

2. a.    b.

3. a.    b.

4. a.    b.

Listen again. Check your answers.

3 After you listen

Talk with a partner. Point to a picture and ask. Your partner says the words.

Who's that?

The grandmother.

☑ Listen for and identify family members   **UNIT 3**   **33**

LESSON **B** Family members

1 Vocabulary focus

Listen and repeat.

CLASS CD1 TK 31

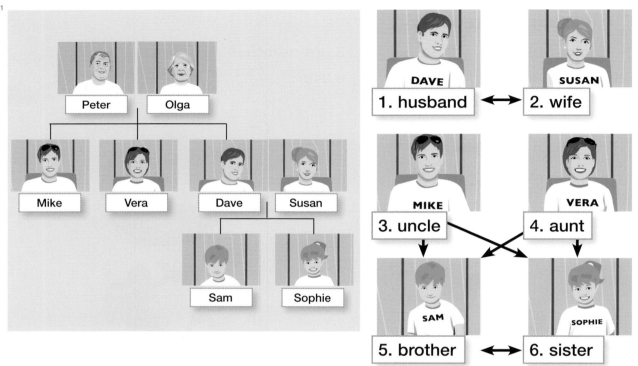

2 Practice

A Read and match.

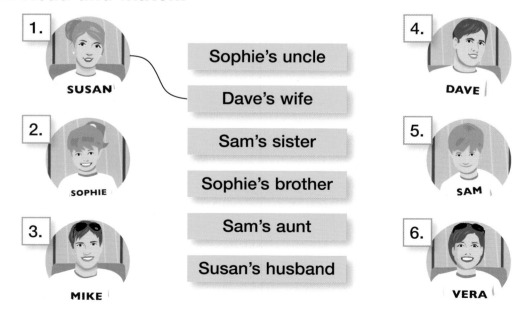

1. SUSAN

Sophie's uncle

Dave's wife

Sam's sister

Sophie's brother

Sam's aunt

Susan's husband

B Listen and repeat. Then write.

CLASS CD1 TK 32

| aunt | brother | husband | sister | uncle | wife |

Who is . . . ?		Who is . . . ?	
1. Vera	Sam's ___aunt___	4. Susan	Dave's _____
2. Mike	Sam's _____	5. Sam	Sophie's _____
3. Sophie	Sam's _____	6. Dave	Susan's _____

Talk with a partner. Ask and answer.

A Who is **Vera**?
B **Sam's aunt.**

3 Communicate

Complete the chart about your family.
Then talk with a partner.

Name	Family member
Habib	brother

A Who is **Habib**?
B My **brother**.

☑ Identify family members   **UNIT 3** **35**

LESSON **C** Do you have a sister?

1 Grammar focus: *Do you have . . . ?*

Questions	Answers	
Do you **have** a sister?	Yes,	I / we	**do**.	No,	I / we	**don't**.

don't = do not

2 Practice

A **Read and circle.** Then write.

1. **A** Do you have a brother?

   B _____*Yes, I do.*_____
   (Yes, I do.) No, I don't.

2. **A** Do you have a sister?

   B _____
   Yes, we do.   No, we don't.

3. **A** Do you have a son?

   B _____
   Yes, I do.   No, I don't.

4. **A** Do you have a daughter?

   B _____
   Yes, we do.   No, we don't.

5. **A** Do you have a wife?

   B _____
   Yes, I do.   No, I don't.

Listen and repeat. Then practice with a partner.

B **Listen and repeat.** Then write.

CLASS CD1 TK 34

Ana

Ken, Danny, and me

Me, Grandma Rose, and Diana

Do you have a . . . ?

1. sister	*yes*
2. brother	
3. husband	

Do you have a . . . ?

4. son	
5. daughter	
6. grandmother	

Talk with a partner. You are Ana. Ask and answer.

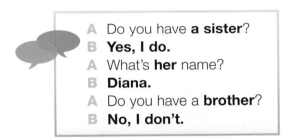

A Do you have **a sister**?
B **Yes, I do.**
A What's **her** name?
B **Diana.**
A Do you have a **brother**?
B **No, I don't.**

3 Communicate

Talk with your classmates. Complete the chart.

Do you have a . . . ?	Dinh					
	Yes	**No**	**Yes**	**No**	**Yes**	**No**
son		✓				
daughter	✓					
sister	✓					
brother	✓					

LESSON **D** Reading

1 Before you read

Talk about the picture. What do you see?

2 Read

 Listen and read.

STUDENT TK 17
CLASS CD1 TK 35

My Family

My name is Gloria. This is my family. This is my mother. Her name is Natalia. It is her birthday. This is my father. His name is Enrico. This is my husband, Luis. We have one daughter. Her name is Lisa. We have one son. His name is Tony. I love my family!

3 After you read

Read and circle. Then write.

1. Luis is Gloria's _____*husband*_____ .
   father (husband)

2. Natalia is Gloria's _____ .
   daughter   mother

3. Tony is Gloria's _____ .
   brother   son

4. Enrico is Gloria's _____ .
   father   mother

5. Lisa is Gloria's _____ .
   sister   daughter

4 **Picture dictionary** People

1. baby
2. girl
3. boy
4. teenager
5. woman
6. man

STUDENT TK 18
CLASS CD1 TK 36

A Listen and repeat. Look at the picture dictionary.

B Talk with a partner. Say a word. Your partner points to the picture.

A Show me the **man**.
B Here's the **man**.

☑ Read a paragraph about a family; use vocabulary for people   **UNIT 3**   **39**

LESSON **E** Writing

1 Before you write

A Talk with a partner. Complete the words.

Frank's Family

1. _d_ a u g h t e r

2. ___ i f e

3. ___ i s t e r

4. ___ a b y

5. ___ o n

6. ___ r o t h e r

Frank

B Talk with a partner. Look at the picture. Complete the story.

My Wonderful Family

My name is Frank. This is my family. This is my ____wife____,
                                                    1

Marie. This is our _____. His name is Patrick. This is our
                        2

_____. Her name is Annie. This is our new _____,
     3   4

Jason. He is a boy. Patrick is his _____. Annie is his
                                        5

_____. I have a wonderful family!
     6

2 Write

A Draw a picture of your family.

B Write about your picture.

| daughter | father | husband | mother | son | wife |

My Wonderful Family

My name is _____ . This is my family.

This is my _____ . _____ name is _____ .
His   Her

This is my _____ . _____ name is _____ .
His   Her

This is my _____ . _____ name is _____ .
His   Her

This is my _____ . _____ name is _____ .
His   Her

I love my family!

3 After you write

Talk with a partner. Share your writing.

LESSON F Another view

1 Life-skills reading

KB **Property Management Company**
230 Central Street, Philadelphia, PA 19019 (215) 555-1863

HOUSING APPLICATION
Directions: Complete the form. Please print.

What is your name? Ali Azari

Who will live with you in the house?

NAME	RELATIONSHIP
Shohreh Azari	wife
Azam Javadi	mother
Omid Azari	son
Navid Azari	son
Fatima Azari	daughter
Leila Azari	daughter
Soraya Azari	daughter

A Read the questions. Look at the housing application.
Fill in the answer.

1. Who is Shohreh Azari?
   - Ⓐ Ali's daughter
   - Ⓑ Ali's wife
   - Ⓒ Ali's son

2. Who is Soraya Azari?
   - Ⓐ Ali's daughter
   - Ⓑ Ali's mother
   - Ⓒ Ali's wife

3. Who is Azam Javadi?
   - Ⓐ Ali's mother
   - Ⓑ Ali's wife
   - Ⓒ Ali's daughter

4. Who is Omid Azari?
   - Ⓐ Ali's brother
   - Ⓑ Ali's father
   - Ⓒ Ali's son

B Talk with a partner. Who lives with you?

2 Fun with vocabulary

A Complete the chart.

an aunt	a father	a man	an uncle
a baby	a girl	a mother	a wife
a boy	a grandfather	a sister	a woman
a brother	a grandmother	a son	
a daughter	a husband	a teenager	

Male	Female	Male or female
	an aunt	

Talk with a partner. Compare your answers.

B Write about yourself. Use the words from 2A.

I am _____ , _____ ,

and _____ .

Talk with a partner. Write about your partner.

My partner _____ is _____ ,

_____ , and _____ .

3 Wrap up

Complete the **Self-assessment** on page 138.

LESSON A
Listening

1 Before you listen

A Look at the picture. What do you see?

B Listen and point: doctor • doctor's office medicine • nurse • patient

CLASS CD1 TK 37

Dr. Brown's Office

Mario

Tony

Unit Goals	Identify health problems
	Interpret a medicine label
	Identify reasons for a visit to a doctor

UNIT 4

2 Listen

A Listen and repeat.

STUDENT TK 19
CLASS CD1 TK 38

1. doctor   2. doctor's office   3. medicine   4. nurse   5. patient

B Listen and circle.

STUDENT TK 20
CLASS CD1 TK 39

1. a.    (b.)

2. a.    b.

3. a.    b.

4. a.    b.

Listen again. Check your answers.

3 After you listen

Talk with a partner. Point to a picture.
Your partner says the word.

LESSON **B** Parts of the body

1 Vocabulary focus

Listen and repeat.

CLASS CD1 TK 40

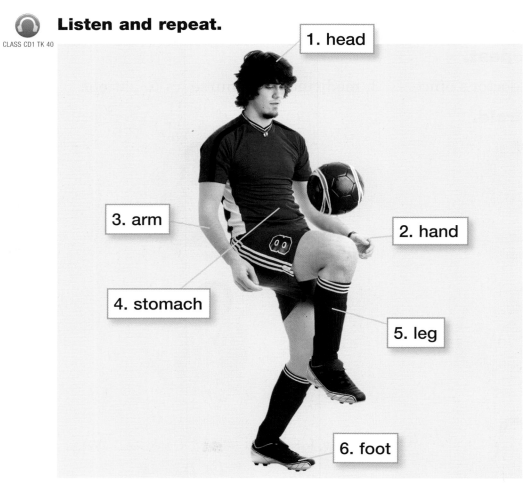

1. head

2. hand

3. arm

4. stomach

5. leg

6. foot

2 Practice

A Read and match.

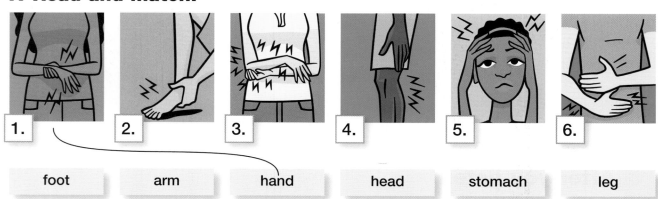

1. 2. 3. 4. 5. 6.

foot   arm   hand   head   stomach   leg

B Listen and repeat. Then write.

CLASS CD1 TK 41

| arm | foot | hand | head | leg | stomach |

What hurts?

1. My ___*hand*___ .   4. My _____ .
2. My _____ .   5. My _____ .
3. My _____ .   6. My _____ .

Talk with a partner. Ask and answer.

A What's the matter?
B My **hand** hurts.

3 Communicate

Talk with a partner.
Act it out. Ask and answer.

What's the matter?

My head hurts.

☑ Use vocabulary for parts of the body   **UNIT 4**   **47**

LESSON C My feet hurt.

1 Grammar focus: singular and plural

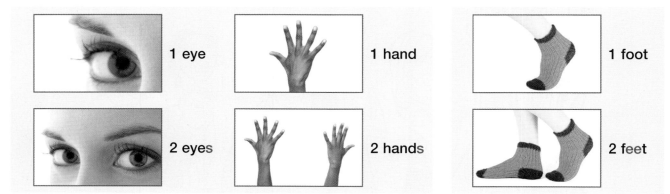

1 eye   1 hand   1 foot

2 eyes   2 hands   2 feet

2 Practice

A Read and circle. Then write.

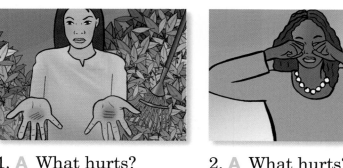

1. A What hurts?

   B My ___hands___ .
      hand (hands)

2. A What hurts?

   B My _____ .
      eye   eyes

3. A What hurts?

   B My _____ .
      arm   arms

4. A What hurts?

   B My _____ .
      foot   feet

5. A What hurts?

   B My _____ .
      leg   legs

6. A What hurts?

   B My _____ .
      hand   hands

Listen and repeat. Then practice with a partner.

CLASS CD1 TK 42

B Listen and repeat.

CLASS CD1 TK 43

1. legs

2. hand

3. stomach

4. feet

5. eyes

6. head

Talk with a partner. Act it out. Ask and answer.

A What hurts?
B My **legs**.
A Oh, I'm sorry.

3 Communicate

Talk with your classmates.
Complete the chart.

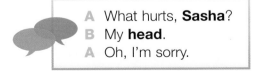
A What hurts, **Sasha**?
B My **head**.
A Oh, I'm sorry.

Name	What hurts?
Sasha	*head*

☑ Use singular and plural nouns   **UNIT 4**   **49**

LESSON **D** Reading

1 **Before you read**

Talk about the picture.
What do you see?

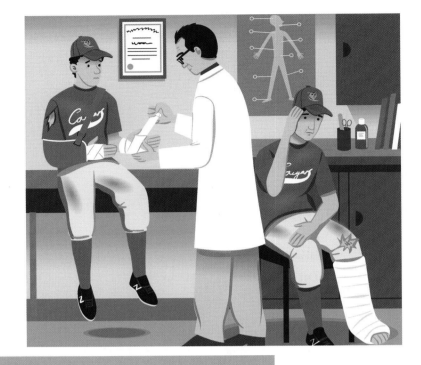

2 **Read**

 Listen and read.

STUDENT TK 21
CLASS CD1 TK 44

At the Doctor's Office

Tony and Mario are at the doctor's office.
They are patients. Tony's leg hurts. His head
hurts, too. He has a headache. Mario's arm
hurts. His hands hurt, too. Tony and Mario are
not happy. It is not a good day.

3 **After you read**

Read the sentences. Check (✓) the names.

	Tony	Mario
His arm hurts.		✓
His head hurts.		
His leg hurts.		
His hands hurt.		
He is not happy.		

4 Picture dictionary Health problems

1. a cold

2. a fever

3. a headache

4. a sore throat

5. a stomachache

6. a toothache

STUDENT TK 22
CLASS CD1 TK 45

A Listen and repeat. Look at the picture dictionary.

B Talk with a partner. Act it out. Ask and answer questions.

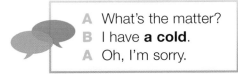

A What's the matter?
B I have **a cold**.
A Oh, I'm sorry.

LESSON **E** Writing

1 Before you write

Talk with a partner. Check (✓) the reason for the visit.

1. Name: *Regina*
Reason for visit:
- ☐ cold
- ☐ fever
- ☐ headache
- ☐ sore throat
- ☐ stomachache
- ☑ toothache

2. Name: *Isaac*
Reason for visit:
- ☐ cold
- ☐ fever
- ☐ headache
- ☐ sore throat
- ☐ stomachache
- ☐ toothache

3. Name: *Joe*
Reason for visit:
- ☐ cold
- ☐ fever
- ☐ headache
- ☐ sore throat
- ☐ stomachache
- ☐ toothache

4. Name: *Esperanza*
Reason for visit:
- ☐ cold
- ☐ fever
- ☐ headache
- ☐ sore throat
- ☐ stomachache
- ☐ toothache

5. Name: *James*
Reason for visit:
- ☐ cold
- ☐ fever
- ☐ headache
- ☐ sore throat
- ☐ stomachache
- ☐ toothache

6. Name: *Sue*
Reason for visit:
- ☐ cold
- ☐ fever
- ☐ headache
- ☐ sore throat
- ☐ stomachache
- ☐ toothache

2 Write

A Talk with a partner. Complete the words.

1. s _o_ re thr _o_ at
2. c ___ l d
3. s t ___ m a c h a c h e
4. h ___ a d a c h e
5. f ___ v e r
6. t ___ o t h a c h e
7. s ___ r e h ___ n d

B Look at page 52. Then complete the patient sign-in sheet.

⚕ Patient Sign-In Sheet

Name of Patient	Reason for Visit
Regina	I have a ____toothache____ .
Isaac	I have a _____ .
Joe	I have a _____ .
Esperanza	I have a _____ .
James	I have a _____ .
Sue	I have a _____ .
_____ (you)	I have a _____ .

3 After you write

Talk with a partner. Share your writing.

LESSON **F** Another view

24 tablets

Colds Away

For relief of colds, headaches, and fevers

Do not use after December 2014.

Do not take more than 8 tablets in 24 hours.

A Read the sentences. Look at the label. Fill in the answer.

1. This medicine is for ____ .
   - Ⓐ a sore throat
   - Ⓑ a stomachache
   - Ⓒ a cold

2. This medicine is for ____ .
   - Ⓐ a headache
   - Ⓑ a backache
   - Ⓒ a toothache

3. This medicine is for ____ .
   - Ⓐ a stomachache
   - Ⓑ a fever
   - Ⓒ a sore throat

4. Do not take this medicine after ____ .
   - Ⓐ 2013
   - Ⓑ 2014
   - Ⓒ 2015

B Talk with a partner.

What is this medicine <u>not</u> for?

2 Fun with vocabulary

A Complete the chart. How many?

	The monster	You
heads	2	1
eyes		
ears		
arms		
legs		
feet		

Talk with a partner. Compare your answers.

B Write the missing letters.

p a t __*i*__ e n t
　　　1

f __＿＿__ e t
　2

s t o __＿＿__ a c h
　　　3

__＿＿__ u r s e
　4

t o o t h a __＿＿__ h e
　　　　　5

__＿＿__ o c t o r
　6

o f f __＿＿__ c e
　　　7

__＿＿__ y e
　8

Write the letters. Make a word.

__＿＿__ __＿＿__ __＿＿__ __*i*__ __＿＿__ __＿＿__ __＿＿__ __＿＿__
　3　　2　　6　　1　　5　　7　　4　　8

3 Wrap up

Complete the **Self-assessment** on page 139.

Review

CLASS CD1 TK 46

Read. Then listen and circle.

1. Who is Sonya?
   a. Tom's aunt
   b. Tom's brother

2. Who is David?
   a. Tom's aunt
   b. Tom's brother

3. Who is Tina?
   a. Ray's sister
   b. Ray's wife

4. Who is Jay?
   a. Barbara's son
   b. Barbara's brother

5. What hurts?
   a. her hand
   b. her head

6. What hurts?
   a. his leg
   b. his foot

Talk with a partner. Ask and answer.

2 Vocabulary

Write. Complete the story.

| cold | doctor's office | medicine | patients | stomach |

A Visit to the Doctor

Marisa and her family are at the _____doctor's office_____.
                                              1

They are _____. Peter is Marisa's son. His
              2

_____ hurts. Antonia is Marisa's daughter. She
      3

has a _____. They need _____. Marisa isn't
           4   5

happy. She has a headache!

3 Grammar

A Read and circle. Then write.

1. What hurts? His _____leg_____.
   (leg) legs

2. What hurts? His _____.
   arm   arms

3. What hurts? Her _____.
   hand   hands

4. What hurts? Her _____.
   foot   feet

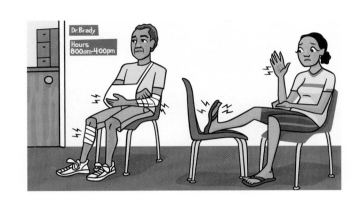

B Complete the sentences. Use *do* or *don't*.

A _____Do_____ you have a daughter?
        1

B Yes, we _____.
              2

A _____ you have a son?
        3

B Yes, we _____.
              4

A _____ you have a sister?
        5

B No, I _____.
              6

4 Pronunciation

CLASS CD1 TK 47

A Listen to the *e* sound, the *i* sound, and the *u* sound.

e   i   u
read   five   June

CLASS CD1 TK 48

B Listen and repeat.

| e | read | need |

| i | five | write |

| u | June | rule |

Talk with a partner. Say a word. Your partner points.
Take turns.

CLASS CD1 TK 49

C Listen and check (✓).

	e	i	u		e	i	u		e	i	u		e	i	u		e	i	u
1.		✓		2.				3.				4.				5.			

LESSON **A**
Listening

1 **Before you listen**

A Look at the picture. What do you see?

CLASS CD1 TK 50

B Listen and point: bank • library • restaurant
school • street • supermarket

Unit Goals
Identify places around town
Identify places on a map
Draw a map and write about it

2 Listen

A Listen and repeat.

STUDENT TK 23
CLASS CD1 TK 51

1. bank   2. library   3. restaurant
4. school   5. street   6. supermarket

B Listen and circle.

STUDENT TK 24
CLASS CD1 TK 52

1. (a.)    b.

2. a.    b.

3. a.    b.

4. a.    b.

Listen again. Check your answers.

3 After you listen

Talk with a partner. Point to a picture.
Your partner says the word.

☑ Listen for and identify places around town   **UNIT 5**   **59**

LESSON **B** Places around town

1 Vocabulary focus

🎧 **Listen and repeat.**

CLASS CD1 TK 53

1. pharmacy

2. hospital

3. laundromat

4. post office

5. movie theater

6. gas station

2 Practice

A Read and match.

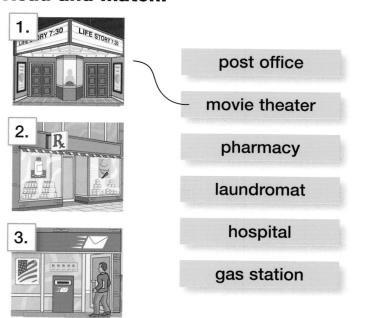

post office

movie theater

pharmacy

laundromat

hospital

gas station

CLASS CD1 TK 54

B Listen and repeat. Then write.

gas station   hospital   laundromat
movie theater   pharmacy   post office

1. Minh

2. Alan

3. Mr. Lopez

4. Paula

5. Jackie

6. Isabel

Name	Place	Name	Place
1. Minh	*movie theater*	4. Paula	
2. Alan		5. Jackie	
3. Mr. Lopez		6. Isabel	

Talk with a partner. Ask and answer.

A Where's **Minh**?
B At the **movie theater**.

3 Communicate

Work in a group. Play a game.
Ask and guess.

A Where is **he**?
B At the **movie theater**?
C That's right!

 Use vocabulary for places around town   **UNIT 5**   **61**

UNIT 5

LESSON C The school is on Main Street.

1 Grammar focus: *on, next to, across from, between*

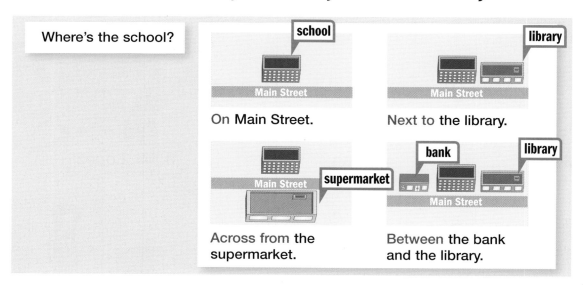

Where's the school?

school — On Main Street.

library — Next to the library.

supermarket — Across from the supermarket.

bank **library** — Between the bank and the library.

2 Practice

A Read and circle. Then write.

1. **A** Where's the pharmacy?

   B _____*Between*_____ the restaurant
   (Between) Across from
   and the supermarket.

2. **A** Where's the supermarket?

   B _____ Main Street.
   Across from   On

3. **A** Where's the restaurant?

   B _____ the pharmacy.
   Between   Next to

4. **A** Where's the bakery?

   B _____ the restaurant.
   Next to   Across from

5. **A** Where's the police station?

   B _____ the bakery.
   On   Next to

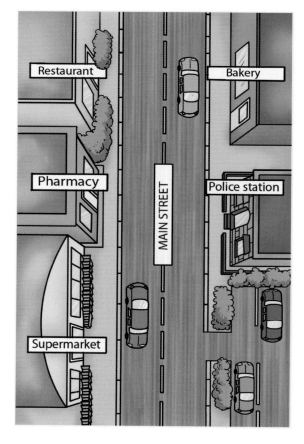

 Listen and repeat. Then practice with a partner.

CLASS CD1 TK 55

B Listen and repeat.

CLASS CD1 TK 56

1. next to

2. across from

3. between

4. on

5. next to

6. across from

Talk with a partner. Ask and answer.

A Excuse me. Where's the **bank**?
B **Next to the supermarket.**
A Thanks.

3 Communicate

Talk with a partner. Play a game.
Ask and guess.

A Where are you?
B **Next to the supermarket.**
A At the **bank**?
B Yes, that's right.

☑ Use *on, next to, across from,* and *between* to describe location   **UNIT 5   63**

LESSON D Reading

1 Before you read

Talk about the picture.
What do you see?

2 Read

Listen and read.

STUDENT TK 25
CLASS CD1 TK 57

Notice from Riverside Library

Come and visit Riverside Library. The new library opens today. The library is on Main Street. It is across from Riverside Adult School. It is next to K and P Supermarket. It is between K and P Supermarket and Rosie's Restaurant. The library is open from 9:00 to 5:00, Monday, Wednesday, and Friday.

3 After you read

Complete the map. Share your map with a partner.

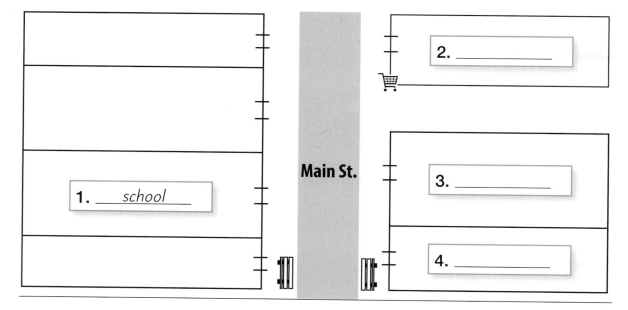

1. _school_

Main St.

2. _____

3. _____

4. _____

4 **Picture dictionary** Transportation

1. by bicycle
2. by bus
3. by car
4. by taxi
5. by train
6. on foot

A Listen and repeat. Look at the picture dictionary.

STUDENT TK 26
CLASS CD1 TK 58 **B Talk with your classmates.** Complete the chart.

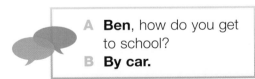

A **Ben**, how do you get to school?
B **By car.**

Name	Transportation
Ben	by car

LESSON E Writing

1 Before you write

A Talk with a partner. Complete the words.

1. s u p e r m a r <u>k</u> e t
2. p ___ a r m a c y
3. p o s t o f ___ i c e
4. r e s ___ a u r a n t
5. l i ___ r a r y
6. s ___ h o o l

B Talk with a partner. Look at the map. Complete the story.

Reed Street

Donna lives on Reed _____<u>Street</u>_____ . She lives near a big
                        1
supermarket. The supermarket is next to a _____ .
                                                              2
A _____ is across from the supermarket. A
                3
<u>p</u>_____ _____ is on Reed Street, too. It is across from
         4
the _____ . A _____ is between the
              5   6
restaurant and the library.

2 Write

A Draw a map of your street.

B Write about your street.

I live on _____ .

I live near a _____ .

A _____ is across from a _____ .

A _____ is between the _____ and

the _____ .

3 After you write

Listen to your partner. Draw your partner's street.

LESSON F Another view

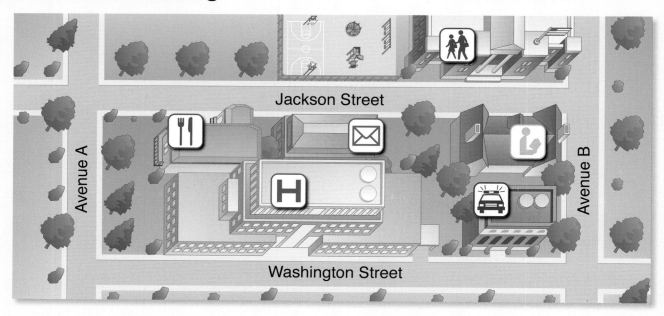

Jackson Street

Avenue A

Avenue B

Washington Street

A Read the sentences. Look at the map. Fill in the answer.

1. The hospital is ____.

   Ⓐ on Jackson Street

   Ⓑ on Washington Street

   Ⓒ on Avenue B

2. The post office is ____.

   Ⓐ next to the police station

   Ⓑ next to the school

   Ⓒ next to the restaurant

3. The post office is ____.

   Ⓐ between the restaurant and the library

   Ⓑ across from the library

   Ⓒ on Washington Street

4. The hospital is ____.

   Ⓐ across from the school

   Ⓑ next to the police station

   Ⓒ between the restaurant and the school

B Talk with a partner about the places on the map.

Where is the police station?
On Washington Street.

Where is the school?
Across from the library.

2 Fun with vocabulary

A Read and match.

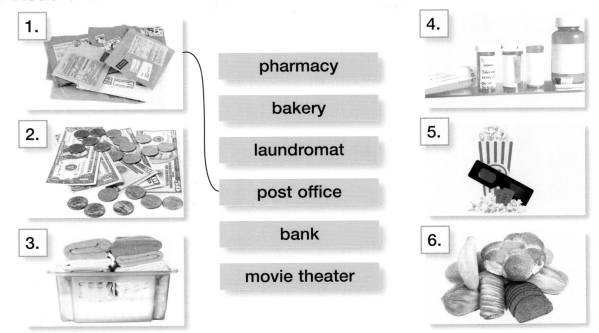

1.

pharmacy

bakery

laundromat

post office

bank

movie theater

2.

3.

4.

5.

6.

Talk with a partner. Check your answers.

B Circle the words in the puzzle.

| bicycle | bus | car | foot | taxi | train |

```
k  f  f  o  o  t  c  s
v  x  a  m  b  r  a  m
k  a  o  t  r  a  i  n
t  a  x  i  s  i  g  t
k  a  v  i  b  u  s  n
b  i  c  y  c  l  e  e
x  r  w  c  a  r  k  b
```

3 Wrap up

Complete the **Self-assessment** on page 140.

LESSON A
Listening

1 Before you listen

A Look at the picture. What do you see?

B Listen and point: 7:00 • 9:00 • 10:00
10:30 • 2:30 • 6:30

CLASS CD2 TK 2

Unit Goals
Read clock time
Make a schedule
Identify parts of an invitation

UNIT 6

2 Listen

A Listen and repeat.

STUDENT TK 27
CLASS CD2 TK 3

1. 7:00   2. 9:00   3. 10:00
4. 10:30   5. 2:30   6. 6:30

B Listen and circle.

STUDENT TK 28
CLASS CD2 TK 4

1. a.    b.

2. a.    b.

3. a.    b.

4. a.    b.

Listen again. Check your answers.

3 After you listen

Talk with a partner.
Point to a picture and ask. Your partner says the time.

USEFUL LANGUAGE

Say times like this.
3:00 = *three o'clock*
6:30 = *six-thirty*

What time is it?

It's 10 o'clock.

LESSON **B** Events

1 Vocabulary focus

🎧 **Listen and repeat.**

SEPTEMBER

Sunday	Monday	Tuesday	Wednesday	Thursday	Friday	Saturday
			1	2	3	4
5	6	7 **1. appointment** 1:30	8	9 **2. meeting**	10 3:30	11
12	13	14 **3. class**	15 page 6 8:30	16	17 **4. movie**	18 7:30
19	20	21	22	23	24	25
26 **5. party** 5:00	27	28	29 **6. TV show** 4:30	30		

2 Practice

A Read and match.

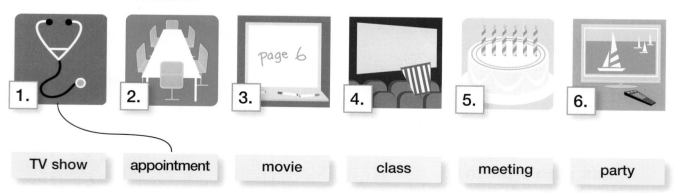

1.   2.   3. page 6   4.   5.   6.

TV show   appointment   movie   class   meeting   party

CLASS CD2 TK 6

B Listen and repeat. Then write.

1.
Town Haircuts

APPOINTMENT INFO:

Day & Time: _Friday 1:30_

Haircut with: _Nick_

2.
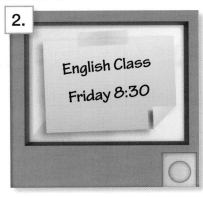
English Class
Friday 8:30

3.

4:30 **Friday**

Channel 3   One Life, One Love
1 hour

Channel 5   Dinosaurs
30 minutes

Channel 7   Afternoon Special
1 hour

4.

RIVERSIDE SCHOOL
PTA MEETING
SATURDAY 3:00

5.

ATTACK FROM VENUS!!
NOW PLAYING: SATURDAY 9:00

6.

You're Invited!
Gina's Birthday Party
Saturday 5:00

Event	Time	Day
appointment	1:30	Friday
TV show		
movie		

Event	Time	Day
class		
party		
meeting		

Talk with a partner. Ask and answer.

A What time is the **appointment**?
B At **1:30** on **Friday**.

3 Communicate

Complete the chart. Write a time and day for each event.
Then talk with your classmates.

Event	Time	Day
movie	7:30	Saturday
TV show		
party		
meeting		

A What time is the **movie**?
B At **7:30** on **Saturday**.

LESSON C Is your class at 11:00?

1 Grammar focus: *Yes / No* questions with *be*

Questions			Answers	
Is	your class	at 11:00?	Yes,	it is.
			No,	it isn't.

isn't = is not

2 Practice

A **Read and circle.** Then write.

Class	Time
English	11:00

November 7

1:00	
1:30	Appointment with: Dr. Martin
2:00	

1. **A** Is your class at 11:00?

   B _____Yes, it is._____
   (Yes, it is.) No, it isn't.

2. **A** Is your appointment at 12:30?

   B _____
   Yes, it is.   No, it isn't.

3. **A** Is your concert at 8:00?

   B _____
   Yes, it is.   No, it isn't.

THE LOST CLUES
6:00

4. **A** Is your movie at 6:00?

   B _____
   Yes, it is.   No, it isn't.

5. **A** Is your party at 4:00?

   B _____
   Yes, it is.   No, it isn't.

Ch. 3	Singing Stars
7:00	Who wins? Final three singers.

6. **A** Is your TV show at 7:30?

   B _____
   Yes, it is.   No, it isn't.

Listen and repeat. Then practice with a partner.

CLASS CD2 TK 7

B Read and match.

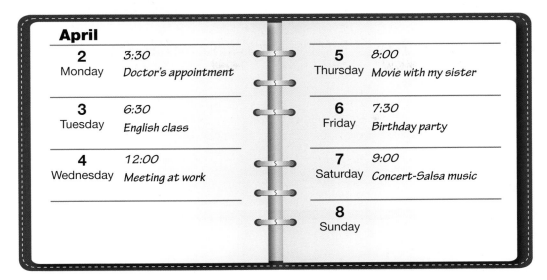

	April				
2 Monday	3:30 Doctor's appointment			**5** Thursday	8:00 Movie with my sister
3 Tuesday	6:30 English class			**6** Friday	7:30 Birthday party
4 Wednesday	12:00 Meeting at work			**7** Saturday	9:00 Concert-Salsa music
				8 Sunday	

1. appointment — seven-thirty
2. class — six-thirty
3. meeting — three-thirty
4. movie — nine o'clock
5. party — twelve o'clock
6. concert — eight o'clock

Talk with a partner. Ask and answer.

A Is your **appointment** on **Monday**?
B **Yes, it is.**
A Is your **appointment** at **7:00**?
B **No, it isn't. It's at 3:30.**

3 Communicate

Complete the chart. Write an event and time for each day.
Then talk with a partner.

appointment   class   concert   meeting   party

Monday	Tuesday	Wednesday	Thursday	Friday
class – 5:00				

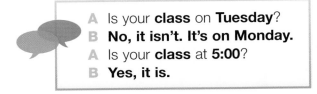

A Is your **class** on **Tuesday**?
B **No, it isn't. It's on Monday.**
A Is your **class** at **5:00**?
B **Yes, it is.**

☑ Use *is* in *yes / no* questions   **UNIT 6**   **75**

LESSON **D** Reading

1 Before you read

Talk about the picture.
What do you see?

2 Read

Listen and read.

STUDENT TK 29
CLASS CD2 TK 8

Teresa's Day

Teresa is busy today. Her meeting with her friend Joan is at 10:00 in the morning. Her doctor's appointment is at 1:00 in the afternoon. Her favorite TV show is at 4:30. Her class is at 6:30 in the evening. Her uncle's birthday party is also at 6:30. Oh, no! What will she do?

3 After you read

Write the answers.

1. What time is Teresa's meeting? _____ *At 10:00* _____.

2. What time is Teresa's TV show? _____.

3. What time is Teresa's class? _____.

4. Is Teresa's appointment at 4:00? _____.

5. Is her uncle's party at 6:30? _____.

4 **Picture dictionary** Times of the day

1. in the morning

2. in the afternoon

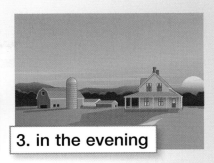
3. in the evening

4. at noon

5. at night

6. at midnight

STUDENT TK 30
CLASS CD2 TK 9

A Listen and repeat. Look at the picture dictionary.

B Talk with a partner. Complete the chart.
Check (✓) the time of the day.

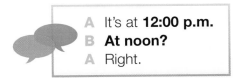

A It's at **12:00 p.m.**
B **At noon?**
A Right.

> **USEFUL** LANGUAGE
>
> a.m. = from midnight to noon
> p.m. = from noon to midnight

	In the morning	In the afternoon	In the evening	At noon	At midnight
12:00 p.m.				✓	
3:00 p.m.					
6:00 a.m.					
12:00 a.m.					
6:00 p.m.					

☑ Read a paragraph about someone's day; use vocabulary for times of the day **UNIT 6** **77**

LESSON E Writing

1 Before you write

A Talk with a partner. Complete the words.

1. m o v _i_ _e_
2. c l a ____ ____
3. a p p ____ ____ n t m e n t
4. p ____ ____ t y
5. TV ____ ____ o w
6. m ____ ____ t i n g

B Talk with a partner. Look at the memo. Complete the story.

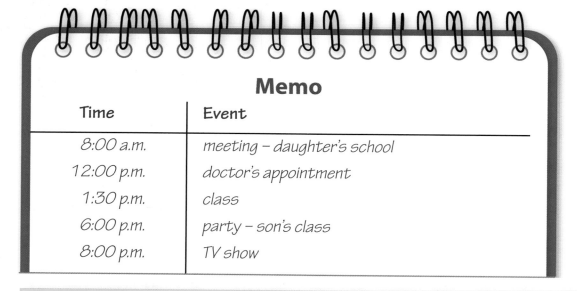

Memo

Time	Event
8:00 a.m.	meeting – daughter's school
12:00 p.m.	doctor's appointment
1:30 p.m.	class
6:00 p.m.	party – son's class
8:00 p.m.	TV show

My Busy Day

Today is a busy day. My ___meeting___ at my daughter's school is

at 8:00 in the morning. Then my doctor's _____ is at noon. My

English _____ is at 1:30. What time is my son's class _____?

Oh, yes. At 6:00 in the evening. Dinner with my family is at 7:00. And

my favorite TV _____ is at 8:00 at night. It's a very busy day.

2 Write

A Complete the memo. Write four times and four events for you.

Memo

Time   Event

_____   _____

_____   _____

_____   _____

_____   _____

B Write about your day.

My Busy Day

Today is a busy day.

My _____ is at _____.

My _____ is at _____.

My _____ is at _____.

And my _____ is at _____.

It's a very busy day.

3 After you write

Talk with a partner. Share your writing.

LESSON F Another view

1 Life-skills reading

It's a party!

Lily is 50! It's her surprise party!
When: *Saturday, October 2*
What time: *8:00 p.m.*
Where: *Katya and Alex's house*
       874 Lake Road
RSVP: *555-6188*

A Read the sentences. Look at the invitation. Fill in the answer.

1. It's a party for ____ .
   - Ⓐ Lily
   - Ⓑ Katya and Alex
   - Ⓒ Katya

2. The party is ____ .
   - Ⓐ in the morning
   - Ⓑ in the afternoon
   - Ⓒ at night

3. The party is at ____ .
   - Ⓐ 2:00 p.m.
   - Ⓑ 4:00 p.m.
   - Ⓒ 8:00 p.m.

4. The party is on ____ .
   - Ⓐ Friday
   - Ⓑ Saturday
   - Ⓒ Sunday

B Talk with a partner about the party.

Tell the day, the time, and the place.

2 Fun with vocabulary

A Write times on the clocks.

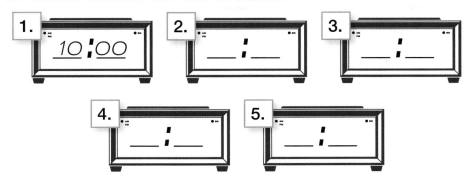

Talk with a partner. Listen and write your partner's times.

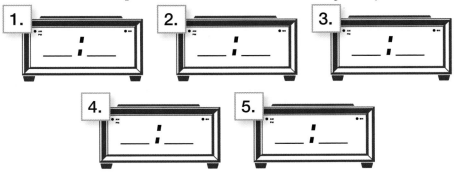

> A What time is it?
> B It's **10:00**.

B Write the missing letters.

$\underset{1}{\underline{d}}$ a y $\qquad \underset{2}{\underline{}}$ o v i e $\qquad$ at n o o $\underset{3}{\underline{}}$ $\qquad$ at n i g $\underset{4}{\underline{}}$ t

in the e v e n $\underset{5}{\underline{}}$ n g $\qquad$ in the a f $\underset{6}{\underline{}}$ e r n o o n

in the m o r n i n $\underset{7}{\underline{}}$ $\qquad$ a p p o $\underset{8}{\underline{}}$ n t m e n t

What time is it? Write the letters below.

$\underset{2}{\underline{}}$ $\underset{8}{\underline{}}$ $\underset{1}{\underline{d}}$ $\underset{3}{\underline{}}$ $\underset{5}{\underline{}}$ $\underset{7}{\underline{}}$ $\underset{4}{\underline{}}$ $\underset{6}{\underline{}}$

3 Wrap up

Complete the **Self-assessment** on page 141.

Review

1 Listening

Read. Then listen and circle.

1. Is the meeting on Friday?
   a. Yes, it is.
   b. No, it isn't.

2. What time is the meeting?
   a. at 2:30
   b. at 10:30

3. What time is the appointment?
   a. at 2:00
   b. at 4:00

4. Where's the school?
   a. next to the bank
   b. across from the bank

5. Where's the movie theater?
   a. between the supermarket and the pharmacy
   b. next to the supermarket

6. Is the movie at 7:30?
   a. Yes, it is.
   b. No, it isn't.

Talk with a partner. Ask and answer.

2 Vocabulary

Write. Complete the story.

| afternoon | class | 8:30 | hospital | meeting |

Tan's Day

Tan's English ___class___ is at _____ in the
                    1   2
morning. His _____ is at 1:00 in the _____.
                  3   4
The meeting is at the _____, next to the school.
                           5
It's a busy day.

3 Grammar

A Read and circle. Then write.

1. The library is ___*across from*___ the bank.
   on (across from)

2. The post office is _____ the bank and the library.
   next to   between

3. The restaurant is _____ Main Street.
   on   between

4. The hospital is _____ the gas station.
   across from   between

B Read the memo and answer. Write *Yes, it is* or *No, it isn't.*

1. Is the movie at 6:00?
   _____*No, it isn't*_____.

2. Is the class at 9:00?
   _____.

3. Is the meeting in the morning?
   _____.

4. Is the appointment in the afternoon?
   _____.

Morning

9:00 class

Afternoon

2:00 – meeting with Ms. Morales

4:30 – appointment with Dr. Morgan

Evening

6:30 – movie

4 Pronunciation

CLASS CD2 TK 11

A Listen to the *a* sound and the *o* sound.

a	o
at	on

CLASS CD2 TK 12

B Listen and repeat.

a	at	class	map		o	on	clock	not

Talk with a partner. Say a word. Your partner points. Take turns.

CLASS CD2 TK 13

C Listen and check (✓).

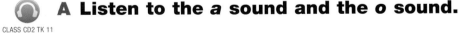

	a	o		a	o		a	o		a	o		a	o
1.		✓	2.			3.			4.			5.		

LESSON A
Listening

1 Before you listen

A Look at the picture. What do you see?

B Listen and point: a dress • pants • a shirt
shoes • socks • a T-shirt

CLASS CD2 TK 14

SUMMER SALE!

THE CLOTHES PLACE

$39.99

$27.00

$19.00

$1.99

$24.99

$10.99

Rose

Samuel

Unit Goals	**Identify** prices
	Complete a shopping list
	Interpret a receipt

2 Listen

A Listen and repeat.

STUDENT TK 31
CLASS CD2 TK 15

1. a dress   2. pants   3. a shirt

4. shoes   5. socks   6. a T-shirt

B Listen and circle.

STUDENT TK 32
CLASS CD2 TK 16

1. (a.)    b.

2. a.    b.

3. a.    b.

4. a.    b.

Listen again. Check your answers.

3 After you listen

Talk with a partner. Point to a picture.
Your partner says the word.

A dress.

☑ Listen for and identify clothing items   **UNIT 7**   **85**

LESSON **B** Clothing

1 Vocabulary focus

CLASS CD2 TK 17

Listen and repeat.

Back-to-School SALE!

1. a tie $10.00
2. a blouse $19.99
3. a sweater $29.99
4. a skirt $24.99
5. a jacket $89.99
6. a raincoat $39.99

2 Practice

A Read and match.

1. 2. 3. 4. 5. 6.

a tie   a blouse   a jacket   a skirt   a raincoat   a sweater

B Listen and repeat. Then write.

blouse   jacket   raincoat   skirt   sweater   tie

1.

The ___tie___ is $9.99.

2.

The _____ is $26.95.

3.

The _____ is $35.95.

4.

The _____ is $39.99.

5.

The _____ is $48.99.

6.

The _____ is $25.95.

Talk with a partner. Ask and answer.

A How much is the **tie**?
B **$9.99.**

3 Communicate

Write prices. Your partner asks the price. You answer.

$ ___24.99___ $ _____ $ _____ $ _____ $ _____

A How much is the **skirt**?
B **$24.99.**

LESSON C How much are the shoes?

1 Grammar focus: *How much is? / How much are?*

Questions			Answers
How much	**is**	the shirt?	$15.99.
	are	the shoes?	$68.95.

2 Practice

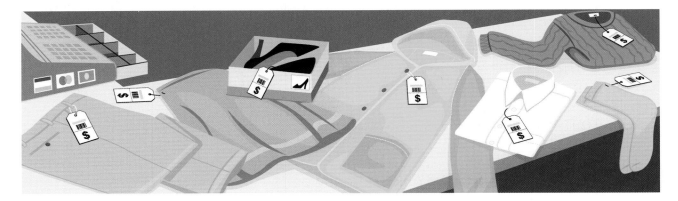

A Read and circle. Then write.

1. A How much _____are_____
   is (are)
   the pants?

   B $24.99.

2. A How much _____
   is   are
   the skirt?

   B $18.99.

3. A How much _____
   is   are
   the raincoat?

   B $16.95.

4. A How much _____
   is   are
   the shoes?

   B $58.99.

5. A How much _____
   is   are
   the sweater?

   B $31.99.

6. A How much _____
   is   are
   the socks?

   B $5.95.

Listen and repeat. Then practice with a partner.

CLASS CD2 TK 19

CLASS CD2 TK 20

B Listen and repeat. Then write.

Yard Sale Today

1. T-shirt $2.00	
2. shoes	
3. jacket	
4. sweater	
5. raincoat	
6. pants	
7. socks	
8. blouse	

Talk with a partner. Ask and answer.

A How much **is the T-shirt**?
B **$2.00.**
A **$2.00?** Thanks.

A How much **are the shoes**?
B **$3.00.**
A **$3.00?** Thanks.

3 Communicate

Write prices. Your partner asks the price. You answer.

$ ___5.00___ $ _____ $ _____ $ _____ $ _____

A How much **are the socks**?
B **$5.00.**

☑ Ask and answer questions about prices   **UNIT 7   89**

LESSON **D** Reading

1 Before you read

Talk about the picture.
What do you see?

2 Read

Listen and read.

STUDENT TK 33
CLASS CD2 TK 21

	New Message
From:	Rose
To:	Patty
Subject:	Shopping

Hi Patty,

This morning, Samuel and I are going to The Clothes Place. Samuel needs blue pants. He needs a tie, too. I need a red dress and black shoes. Dresses are on sale. They're $49.99. Shoes are on sale, too. They're $34.99. That's good.

Call you later,

Rose

3 After you read

Read and match.

1.

2.

Samuel needs blue pants.

Samuel needs a tie.

Dresses are on sale.

Shoes are on sale.

3.

4.

4 Picture dictionary Colors

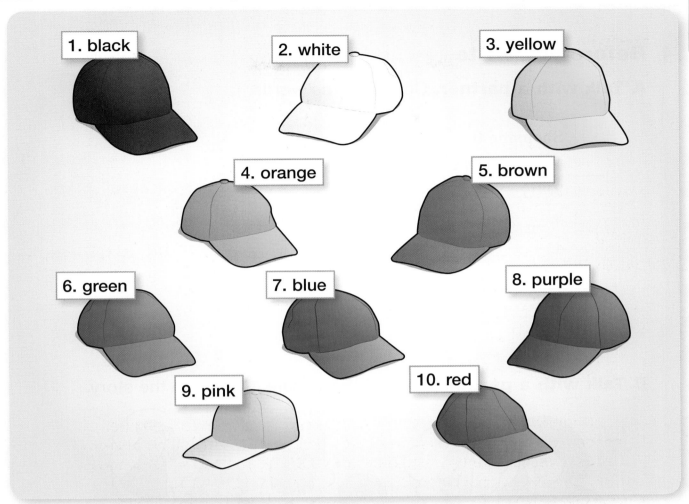

1. black
2. white
3. yellow
4. orange
5. brown
6. green
7. blue
8. purple
9. pink
10. red

STUDENT TK 34
CLASS CD2 TK 22

A Listen and repeat. Look at the picture dictionary.

B Talk with a partner. Look around your classroom. Ask and answer.

A What color is **her sweater**?
B **Blue.**

A What color are **his shoes**?
B **Brown.**

C Talk with a partner. Choose four classmates. Complete the chart.

Name	red	yellow	green	black	white	brown	blue
Eliza	sweater	socks			blouse		

☑ Read an e-mail about a shopping trip; name colors **UNIT 7 91**

LESSON E Writing

1 Before you write

A Talk with a partner. Complete the words.

Shopping list
1. _s_ _k_ i r t
2. ___ ___ e s s
3. ___ ___ o e s
4. ___ ___ o u s e
5. ___ ___ e a t e r
6. T- ___ ___ i r t

B Talk with a partner. Look at the picture. Complete the story.

Sun Mi and her children are shopping today. They

need clothes for school. Sun Mi needs a ___*dress*___ and
                                            1

_____ . Her son Roger needs a _____ and a
      2   3

_____ . Her daughter Emily needs a _____ and
      4   5

a _____ .
     6

2 Write

A Complete the shopping list for Sun Mi's family.

Name	Clothing
Sun Mi:	a dress,
Emily:	
Roger:	

B Circle the clothes you and your family need.

a blouse	socks	a tie	a dress
a sweater	a jacket	a skirt	a raincoat
a T-shirt	a shirt	shoes	pants

C Write a shopping list for your family.

Name	Clothing

3 After you write

Talk with a partner. Share your writing.

LESSON **F** Another view

the
Clothes
Place

271 Center Street
Tampa, Florida 33601
(813) 555-7200

Shoes	$29.99
T-shirt	$7.99
Subtotal:	$37.98
7% Tax:	$2.66
Total:	**$40.64**

Thank you for shopping at
The Clothes Place.
Have a nice day!

A Read the sentences. Look at the receipt. Fill in the answer.

1. The Clothes Place is a ____.
   Ⓐ clothing store
   Ⓑ supermarket
   Ⓒ laundromat

2. The phone number is ____.
   Ⓐ 555-0072
   Ⓑ 555-7200
   Ⓒ 813

3. The shoes are ____.
   Ⓐ $29.99
   Ⓑ $19.99
   Ⓒ $40.64

4. The tax is ____.
   Ⓐ $40.64
   Ⓑ $37.98
   Ⓒ $2.66

B Talk with a partner.

1. Where do you buy clothes?
2. What clothes do you need?

2 Fun with vocabulary

Write the words in the puzzle. Some words are across (→).
Some words are down (↓).

Across →

Down ↓

3 Wrap up

Complete the **Self-assessment** on page 142.

LESSON **A**
Listening

1 Before you listen

A Look at the picture. What do you see?

B Listen and point: cashier • custodian • mechanic receptionist • salesperson • server

CLASS CD2 TK 23

Unit Goals	Identify jobs
	Identify job duties
	Interpret help wanted ads

2 Listen

A Listen and repeat.

STUDENT TK 35
CLASS CD2 TK 24

1. cashier   2. custodian   3. mechanic

4. receptionist   5. salesperson   6. server

B Listen and circle.

STUDENT TK 36
CLASS CD2 TK 25

1. a.    b.

2. a.    b.

3. a.    b.

4. a.    b.

Listen again. Check your answers.

3 After you listen

Talk with a partner. Point to a picture.
Your partner says the word.

LESSON **B** Job duties

1 Vocabulary focus

Listen and repeat.

CLASS CD2 TK 26

1. She answers the phone.

2. She counts money.

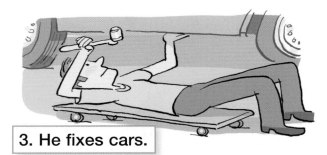

3. He fixes cars.

4. He cleans buildings.

5. She sells clothes.

6. He serves food.

2 Practice

A Read and match.

1. A receptionist   sells clothes.
2. A salesperson   cleans buildings.
3. A cashier   answers the phone.
4. A server   fixes cars.
5. A custodian   serves food.
6. A mechanic   counts money.

B Listen and repeat. Then write.

CLASS CD2 TK 27

| answers the phone | cleans buildings | counts money |
| fixes cars | sells clothes | serves food |

Stephanie

Sandra

DOCTOR'S OFFICE

Alba

Tim

Oscar

PRIVATE

Ahmad

Name	Duty		Name	Duty
1. Sandra	She _____counts money_____ .		4. Oscar	He _____ .
2. Stephanie	She _____ .		5. Tim	He _____ .
3. Alba	She _____ .		6. Ahmad	He _____ .

Talk with a partner. Ask and answer.

A What does **Sandra** do?
B **She counts money.**

3 Communicate

Talk with your classmates. Ask and answer.

A What do you do?
B I'm a **cashier. I count money.**

USEFUL LANGUAGE

What do you do? =
What's your job?

☑ Use vocabulary for jobs and job duties **UNIT 8** **99**

LESSON C Does he sell clothes?

1 Grammar focus: *does* and *doesn't*

Questions			Answers						
Does	he	sell clothes?	Yes,	he	**does**.	No,	he	**doesn't**.
	she			she			she	

doesn't = does not

2 Practice

A Read and circle. Then write.

1. **A** Does he serve food?

   B No, he ___doesn't___ .
   does (doesn't)

2. **A** Does he clean buildings?

   B Yes, he _____ .
   does   doesn't

3. **A** Does she answer the phone?

   B Yes, she _____ .
   does   doesn't

4. **A** Does he sell clothes?

   B Yes, he _____ .
   does   doesn't

5. **A** Does she fix cars?

   B No, she _____ .
   does   doesn't

Listen and repeat. Then practice with a partner.

CLASS CD2 TK 28

CLASS CD2 TK 29

B **Listen and repeat.** Then write.

1. **A** ___Does___ he ___sell___ clothes?

   B ___No___ , he ___doesn't___ .

2. **A** _____ he _____ cars?

   B _____ , he _____ .

3. **A** _____ he _____ buildings?

   B _____ , he _____ .

4. **A** _____ he _____ food?

   B _____ , he _____ .

5. **A** _____ he _____ money?

   B _____ , he _____ .

6. **A** _____ he _____ the phone?

   B _____ , he _____ .

Talk with a partner. Ask and guess his job.

cashier	custodian
mechanic	receptionist
salesperson	server

A What's his job?
B He's a _____ .

Communicate

Talk with your classmates. Play a game.
Ask and guess.

A Do you **sell clothes**?
B **No.**
A Do you **fix cars**?
B **Yes.**
A You're a **mechanic**?
B **Yes, that's right.**

☑ Use *does* and *doesn't* in *yes / no* questions and short answers   **UNIT 8**   **101**

LESSON **D** Reading

1 Before you read

Talk about the picture.
What do you see?

2 Read

 Listen and read.

STUDENT TK 37
CLASS CD2 TK 30

Employee of the Month:
Sara Lopez

Congratulations, Sara Lopez – Employee of the Month! Sara is a salesperson. She sells clothes. Sara's whole family works here at Shop Smart. Her father is a custodian, and her mother is a receptionist. Her Uncle Eduardo is a server. He serves food. Her sister Lucy is a cashier. She counts money. Her brother Leo fixes cars. He's a mechanic. Everybody in the store knows the Lopez family!

3 After you read

Write the job and the job duty.

1.
Name	Job
Leo Lopez	mechanic

Job duty

He fixes cars. $hop $mart

2.
Name	Job
Lucy Lopez	

Job duty

                              $hop $mart

3.
Name	Job
Eduardo Lopez	

Job duty

                              $hop $mart

4.
Name	Job
Sara Lopez	

Job duty

                              $hop $mart

4 **Picture dictionary** Jobs

1. bus driver
SCHOOL BUS

2. homemaker

3. painter

4. plumber

5. teacher's aide
14+12=
8=

6. truck driver

STUDENT TK 38
CLASS CD2 TK 31

A Listen and repeat. Look at the picture dictionary.

B Talk with a partner. Point and ask. Your partner answers.

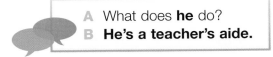

A What does **he** do?
B **He's a teacher's aide.**

LESSON E Writing

1 Before you write

A Talk with a partner. Check (✓) the job duty.

	Counts money	Drives a bus	Cleans buildings	Answers the phone	Serves food
cashier	✓				
custodian					
server					
bus driver					
receptionist					

B Talk with a partner. Complete the words.

1. s a l e s p _e_ _r_ s o n
2. s e l l s ___ ___ o t h e s
3. m e ___ ___ a n i c
4. f i x ___ ___ c a r s
5. a n ___ ___ e r s t h e p h o n e
6. c ___ ___ n t s m o n e y

C Read the letter.

Dear Grandpa,

How are you? We are all well here. Luis and Maria have new jobs! Luis is a server. He serves food. Maria is a receptionist. She answers the phone. I'm a homemaker. I work at home. Write soon.

Love,
Rosa

2 Write

A Talk with a partner. Complete the letter. Use the words from 1B.

Dear Grandma,

How are you? We are all well here. Janie and Walter have new jobs!

Janie is a _salesperson_. She _____ clothes. She also
           1   2

_____ the phone at work, and she _____ money. Walter is
   3   4

a _____. He _____ cars.
   5   6

Write soon.

Love,
Meg

B Write about your family and friends. Write about their jobs.

My ___friend's___ name is ___Sandra___.
She is a ___receptionist___. She ___answers the phone___.

1. My _____'s name is _____.
He is a _____. He _____.

2. My _____'s name is _____.
She is a _____. She _____.

3. My _____'s name is _____.
_____ is a _____.
_____.

3 After you write

Talk with a partner. Share your writing.

LESSON F Another view

Help Wanted

JOB A
Salesperson
$15.00 an hour
Monday and Wednesday
Call 555-1188

JOB B
Painter
Acme Paint Company
Call 555-8491
Part-time work

JOB C
Cashier
$12.00 an hour
Shop Smart
E-mail: ShopSmart@cup.org

JOB D
Bus Driver
City Bus Company
Work mornings
Call evenings
555-7654

A Read the sentences. Look at the ads. Fill in the answer.

1. Job A is for a ____ .
   Ⓐ cashier
   Ⓑ receptionist
   Ⓒ salesperson

2. Job B is for a ____ .
   Ⓐ driver
   Ⓑ painter
   Ⓒ plumber

3. For Job C, ____ .
   Ⓐ write to Shop Smart
   Ⓑ go to Shop Smart
   Ⓒ call Shop Smart

4. Call City Bus Company ____ .
   Ⓐ in the morning
   Ⓑ in the afternoon
   Ⓒ in the evening

B Talk with a partner.

What job do you want?

2 Fun with vocabulary

A Read and match.

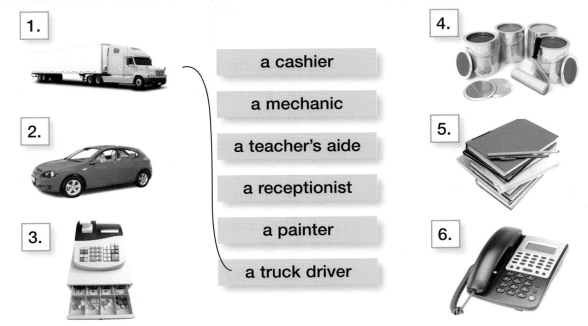

1.

2.

3.

a cashier

a mechanic

a teacher's aide

a receptionist

a painter

a truck driver

4.

5.

6.

Talk with a partner. Check your answers.

B Circle the words in the puzzle.

answer	cashier	clean	count	custodian
fix	mechanic	sell	server	

```
t   f   i   x   a   b   c   o   u   n   t   q

f   g   m   e   c   h   a   n   i   c   r   o

s   e   r   v   e   r   c   c   l   e   a   n

d   s   e   a   n   s   w   e   r   u   b   a

s   e   l   l   c   a   s   h   i   e   r

t   r   c   u   s   t   o   d   i   a   n   r
```

3 Wrap up

Complete the **Self-assessment** on page 143.

Review

1 Listening

CLASS CD2 TK 32

Read. Then listen and circle.

1. What does Chul do?
   (a.) He's a cashier.
   b. He's a custodian.

2. Does he serve food?
   a. Yes, he does.
   b. No, he doesn't.

3. What does Luz do?
   a. She's a salesperson.
   b. She's a receptionist.

4. Does she answer the phone?
   a. Yes, she does.
   b. No, she doesn't.

5. What color are the pants?
   a. blue
   b. green

6. How much are the pants?
   a. $9.99
   b. $19.99

Talk with a partner. Ask and answer.

2 Vocabulary

Write. Complete the story.

| cars | clothes | mechanic | $9.99 | salesperson | shirt |

A New Shirt

Sam is a __mechanic__. He fixes _____. Today he
               1   2

is at Shop Smart. He needs a blue _____. Shirts are
                               3

on sale. Brenda is a _____. She sells _____ at
               4   5

Shop Smart. How much is the shirt? It's _____.
                                   6

3 Grammar

A Complete the sentences. Use *is* or *are*.

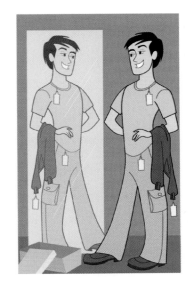

1. **A** How much _____*is*_____ the T-shirt?

   B $10.99.

2. **A** How much _____ the pants?

   B $28.99.

3. **A** How much _____ the shoes?

   B $39.95.

4. **A** How much _____ the sweater?

   B $22.95.

B Read and circle. Then write.

1. **A** Does Kayla count money?

   B Yes, she _____*does*_____ .
      (does) doesn't

2. **A** Does she clean buildings?

   B No, she _____ .
      does   doesn't

3. **A** Does Allen fix cars?

   B No, he _____ .
      does   doesn't

4. **A** Does he serve food?

   B Yes, he _____ .
      does   doesn't

4 Pronunciation

A Listen to the *e* sound, the *i* sound, and the *u* sound.

CLASS CD2 TK 33

e	i	u
red	six	bus

B Listen and repeat.

CLASS CD2 TK 34

e	red	when

i	six	his

u	bus	much

Talk with a partner. Say a word. Your partner points. Take turns.

C Listen and check (✓).

CLASS CD2 TK 35

	e	i	u		e	i	u		e	i	u		e	i	u		e	i	u
1.	✓			2.				3.				4.				5.			

LESSON **A**
Listening

1 **Before you listen**

A Look at the picture. What do you see?

B Listen and point: doing homework • doing the laundry • drying the dishes • making lunch • making the bed • washing the dishes

CLASS CD2 TK 36

Unit Goals
Identify family chores
Complete a chart about family chores
Interpret a work order

UNIT 9

2 Listen

A Listen and repeat.

STUDENT TK 39
CLASS CD2 TK 37

1. doing homework
2. doing the laundry
3. drying the dishes
4. making lunch
5. making the bed
6. washing the dishes

B Listen and circle.

STUDENT TK 40
CLASS CD2 TK 38

1. (a.) 　b.

2. a. 　b.

3. a. 　b.

4. a. 　b.

Listen again. Check your answers.

3 After you listen

Talk with a partner. Point to a picture.
Your partner says the words.

LESSON **B** Outside chores

1 Vocabulary focus

Listen and repeat.

CLASS CD2 TK 39

1. cutting the grass

2. getting the mail

3. taking out the trash

4. walking the dog

5. washing the car

6. watering the grass

2 Practice

A Read and match.

| taking out the trash | washing the car | cutting the grass |

 1.

 2.

 3.

| watering the grass | getting the mail | walking the dog |

B Listen and repeat. Then write.

Name	Chore
1. Mrs. Navarro	_watering_ the grass
2. Mr. Navarro	_____ the grass
3. Roberto	_____ the car
4. Diego	_____ _____ the trash
5. Norma	_____ the mail
6. Rita	_____ the dog

Talk with a partner. Ask and answer.

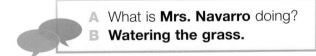

A What is **Mrs. Navarro** doing?
B **Watering the grass.**

3 Communicate

Talk with a partner. Act and guess.

That's right.

Watering the grass?

☑ Use vocabulary for outside chores **UNIT 9** **113**

LESSON C What are they doing?

1 Grammar focus: questions with *What*

Questions				Answers
	is	he		**Cutting** the grass.
What	**is**	she	**doing**?	**Walking** the dog.
	are	they		**Washing** the dishes.

2 Practice

A Read and circle. Then write.

1. A What _____are_____ they doing?
   <u>is (are)</u>
   B Making dinner.

   A What _____ he doing?
   <u>is   are</u>
   B Washing the dishes.

2. A What _____ they doing?
   <u>is   are</u>
   B Making the bed.

   A What _____ he doing?
   <u>is   are</u>
   B Taking out the trash.

3. A What _____ he doing?
   <u>is   are</u>
   B Washing the car.

   A What _____ she doing?
   <u>is   are</u>
   B Watering the grass.

Listen and repeat. Then practice with a partner.

CLASS CD2 TK 41

CLASS CD2 TK 42

B Listen and repeat. Then write.

cutting	doing	drying	getting	making	taking

1. __*getting*__ the mail

2. _____ lunch.

3. _____ the grass.

4. _____ the laundry.

5. _____ the dishes.

6. _____ out the trash.

Talk with a partner. Ask and answer.

A What **are they** doing?
B **Getting the mail.**

A What **is he** doing?
B **Making lunch.**

3 Communicate

Talk with a partner. Make a picture. Ask and guess.

What are they doing?   Drying the dishes.

☑ Ask and answer questions with *What* (*What is she doing?*)   UNIT 9   **115**

LESSON **D** Reading

1 Before you read

Talk about the picture.
What do you see?

2 Read

Listen and read.

New Message

From: Huan

To: Susie

Subject: Help

Dear Susie,

It's after dinner. My family is working in the kitchen. My daughter Li is washing the dishes. My daughter Mei is drying the dishes. My husband and Tao are taking out the trash. Where is my oldest son? He isn't in the kitchen. He is sleeping in the living room! I am not happy.

I need help. What can I do?

Huan

3 After you read

Read and match.

1.

2.

They are taking out the trash.

She is drying the dishes.

She is washing the dishes.

She is not happy.

3.

4.

4 **Picture dictionary** Rooms of a house

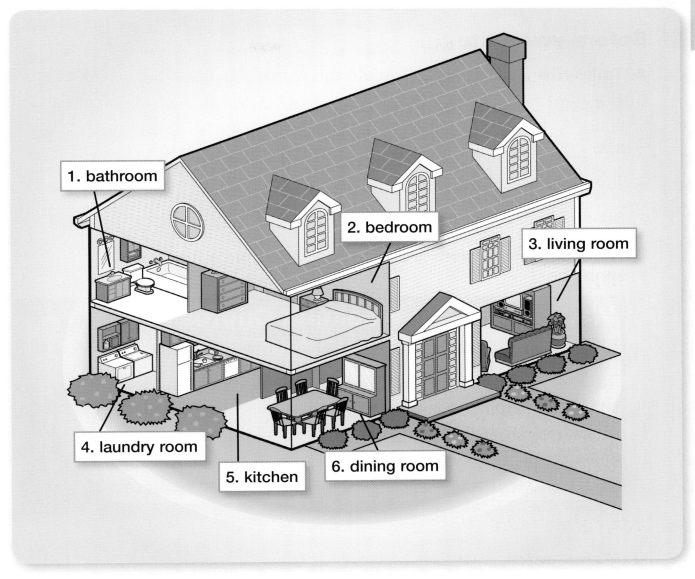

1. bathroom
2. bedroom
3. living room
4. laundry room
5. kitchen
6. dining room

STUDENT TK 42
CLASS CD2 TK 44

A **Listen and repeat.** Look at the picture dictionary.

B **Talk with a partner.** Point to a room and ask. Your partner answers.

A What room is this?
B **The kitchen.**

☑ **Read about problems with family chores; name rooms of a house** **UNIT 9** **117**

LESSON **E** Writing

1 Before you write

A Talk with a partner. Complete the words.

1. d _o_ i _n_ _g_   the   _l_ a u n _d_ r _y_
2. m ___ k ___ n g   the   ___ e ___ s
3. w ___ l ___ i n g   the   ___ o ___
4. c ___ t t ___ n g   the   ___ r a ___ s
5. w ___ s ___ i n g   the   ___ i s ___ e s
6. t ___ k i n g   o u t   t h e   ___ r a s ___

B Talk with a partner. Read the chart. Complete the sentences.

Walker Family's Weekend Chores

Chore	Dad	Mom	Max	Iris	Charlie
Do the laundry.		✔		✔	
Take out the trash.					✔
Wash the dishes.			✔		
Cut the grass.	✔				
Make the beds.		✔			
Walk the dog.			✔		✔

It is the weekend. We are doing chores.

1. Charlie is _____ _taking_ _____ _out_ ___ _the_ _____ _trash_ _____.

2. Mom and Iris are _____ ____ _____.

3. Dad is _____ ____ _____.

4. Max is _____ ____ _____.

5. Mom is _____ ____ _____.

6. Charlie and Max are _____ ____ _____.

2 Write

A **Complete the chart.** Write the weekend chores at your house. Write your family's names. Check (✓) the names.

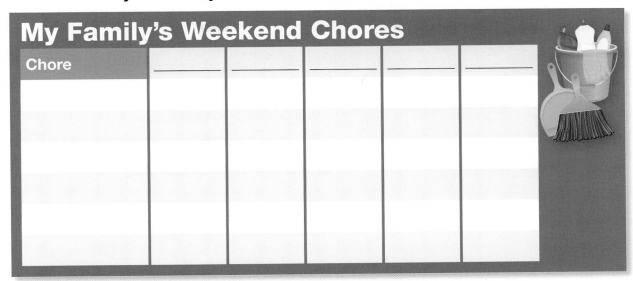

My Family's Weekend Chores

Chore	_____	_____	_____	_____	_____

B **Write.** It is the weekend. Tell about your family's chores. Look at 1B for help.

It is the weekend. We are doing chores.

1. I am _____.

2. _____ is _____.

3. _____ is _____.

4. _____ is _____.

5. _____ and _____ are _____.

3 After you write

Talk with a partner. Share your writing.

LESSON F Another view

1 Life-skills reading

Friendly Cleaning Service, Inc.
Madison, WI 53714

We do your chores with a smile!

Work Order for:

1812 Franklin Street

Date: Monday, August 27

Madison, WI 53714

Name	Chore
Alma	dishes
Kay	beds
Ramiro	grass
Cyrus	laundry
Binh	trash

A **Read the sentences.** Look at the work order. Fill in the answer.

1. Alma's chore is ____ .
   - Ⓐ cutting the grass
   - Ⓑ washing the dishes
   - Ⓒ making the beds

2. Kay's chore is ____ .
   - Ⓐ making the beds
   - Ⓑ doing the laundry
   - Ⓒ washing the dishes

3. Ramiro's chore is ____ .
   - Ⓐ doing the laundry
   - Ⓑ taking out the trash
   - Ⓒ cutting the grass

4. Binh's chore is ____ .
   - Ⓐ doing the laundry
   - Ⓑ cutting the grass
   - Ⓒ taking out the trash

B **Talk with a partner.**

What are your chores?

2 Fun with vocabulary

A Talk with a partner. Complete the chart.

the bed	the car	the dishes	the dog
the grass	homework	the laundry	lunch

cut	wash	do	make	dry
			the bed	

B Circle eight **-ing** words in the puzzle.

```
e   j   d   y   s   w   a   l   k   i   n   g   r   f   t
s   z   w   a   t   e   r   i   n   g   a   r   t   a   j
v   s   b   b   n   l   k   z   w   a   s   h   i   n   g
e   a   g   u   g   o   z   m   a   k   i   n   g   e   t
g   e   t   t   i   n   g   e   h   t   w   i   v   i   i
k   r   c   b   m   z   d   r   y   i   n   g   h   g   x
c   u   t   t   i   n   g   w   m   m   b   c   a   a   f
h   c   l   t   a   k   i   n   g   d   o   p   n   g   g
```

3 Wrap up

Complete the **Self-assessment** on page 144.

10 Free time

LESSON **A**
Listening

1 **Before you listen**

A Look at the picture. What do you see?

B Listen and point: dance • exercise • fish
play basketball • play cards • swim

CLASS CD2 TK 45

Jane

Exercise Station

Dan

Jack

Lupe

Unit Goals	**Identify** free-time activities
	Describe what people like to do
	Interpret information on a class flyer

2 Listen

A Listen and repeat.

STUDENT TK 43
CLASS CD2 TK 46

1. dance   2. exercise   3. fish

4. play basketball   5. play cards   6. swim

B Listen and circle.

STUDENT TK 44
CLASS CD2 TK 47

1. (a.)    b.

2. a.    b.

3. a.    b.

4. a.    b.

Listen again. Check your answers.

3 After you listen

Talk with a partner. Point to a picture.
Your partner says the words.

LESSON **B** Around the house

1 Vocabulary focus

🎧 **Listen and repeat.**

CLASS CD2 TK 48

1. cook

2. play the guitar

3. listen to music

4. watch TV

5. read magazines

6. work in the garden

2 Practice

A Read and match.

work in the garden	play the guitar	cook

1.   2.   3.

watch TV	listen to music	read magazines

CLASS CD2 TK 49

B Listen and repeat. Then write.

| cook | listen to music | play the guitar |
| read magazines | watch TV | work in the garden |

Name	Activity	Name	Activity
1. Pablo	*watch TV*	4. Estela	
2. Tom		5. Ling	
3. Rashid		6. Farah	

Talk with a partner. Ask and answer.

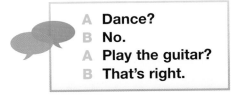

A What does **Pablo** like to do?
B **Watch TV.**

3 Communicate

Talk with a partner. Act and guess.

A Dance?
B No.
A Play the guitar?
B That's right.

LESSON C I like to watch TV.

1 Grammar focus: *like to*

Questions				Answers		
	do	you		I	**like**	
What	**do**	they	**like to** do?	They	**like**	**to** watch TV.
	does	he		He	**likes**	
	does	she		She	**likes**	

2 Practice

A Read and circle. Then write.

1. **A** What do they like to do?

   B They _____*like*_____ to play basketball.
   (like) likes

2. **A** What does she like to do?

   B She _____ to swim.
   like   likes

3. **A** What does he like to do?

   B He _____ to play cards.
   like   likes

4. **A** What does she like to do?

   B She _____ to fish.
   like   likes

5. **A** What do they like to do?

   B They _____ to dance.
   like   likes

Listen and repeat. Then practice with a partner.

CLASS CD2 TK 50

B Listen and repeat.

CLASS CD2 TK 51

1. exercise

2. cook

3. play cards

4. work in the garden

5. swim

6. play soccer

Talk with a partner. Ask and answer.

A What **does he** like to do?
B **He likes to exercise.**

3 Communicate

Talk with your classmates. Complete the chart.

A What do you like to do, **Vinh**?
B I like to **play basketball**.

Name	What do you like to do?
Vinh	play basketball

☑ Use the simple present of *like to* **UNIT 10** **127**

LESSON **D** Reading

1 Before you read

Talk about the picture.
What do you see?

2 Read

Listen and read.

STUDENT TK 45
CLASS CD2 TK 52

New Message

From: Lupe

To: Miriam

Subject: Call me

Hi Miriam,

I'm not working today. It's my day off. Are you busy? Come and visit me!

What do you like to do? I like to cook. I like to play cards. I like to listen to music and dance. I like to watch TV. Do you like to watch TV?

Please call me at 10:00.

See you soon!

Lupe

---

3 After you read

Check (✓) the answers. What does Lupe like to do?

1. ☐   2. ☐   3. ☐   4. ☐   5. ☐

4 **Picture dictionary** Free-time activities

1. go to the movies
2. go online
3. shop

BIG SHOE SALE!
TODAY ONLY!

4. travel
5. visit friends
6. volunteer

VOLUNTEER
CLEANUP

STUDENT TK 46
CLASS CD2 TK 53

A Listen and repeat. Look at the picture dictionary.

B Talk with a partner. Point and ask. Your partner answers.

A What do they like to do?
B **Go to the movies.**

LESSON **E** Writing

1 Before you write

A Talk with a partner. Complete the words.

1. r _e_ _a_ d   m _a_ g a z i n e s
2. p l ___ y   b ___ s k ___ t b a l l
3. w ___ t c h   T V
4. v ___ s ___ t   f r i ___ n d s
5. ___ x ___ r c ___ s e
6. w ___ r k   ___ n   t h e   g a r d ___ n

B Talk with a partner. Write the words.

1. ___exercise___

2. _____ magazines

3. _____ basketball

4. _____ in the garden

5. _____ friends

6. _____ TV

2 Write

A Complete the sentences. Look at 1B.

My name is Brian.

Saturday is my day off.

1. I like to _____exercise_____ in the morning.
2. I like to _____ magazines, too.
3. I like to _____ basketball with my son in the afternoon.
4. I also like to _____ in the garden.
5. I like to _____ friends in the evening.
6. I like to _____ TV at night.

B Check (✓). What do you like to do on your day off?

☐ cook   ☐ play cards
☐ dance   ☐ shop
☐ exercise   ☐ swim
☐ fish   ☐ volunteer
☐ go to the movies   ☐ other: _____

Write about yourself.

My Day Off

My name is _____.

_____ is my day off.

I like to _____.

I like to _____.

I like to _____.

I like to _____.

3 After you write

Talk with a partner. Share your writing.

LESSON F Another view

Life-skills reading

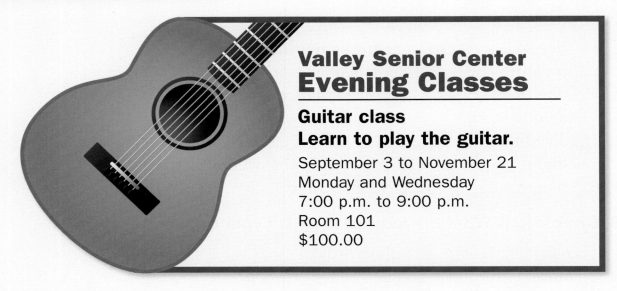

Valley Senior Center
Evening Classes

Guitar class
Learn to play the guitar.
September 3 to November 21
Monday and Wednesday
7:00 p.m. to 9:00 p.m.
Room 101
$100.00

A Read the sentences. Look at the class description.
Fill in the answer.

1. This description is for _____ .
   - Ⓐ a guitar class
   - Ⓑ an exercise class
   - Ⓒ an ESL class

2. The class is in Room _____ .
   - Ⓐ 100
   - Ⓑ 101
   - Ⓒ 901

3. The class is in the _____ .
   - Ⓐ morning
   - Ⓑ afternoon
   - Ⓒ evening

4. The class is _____ .
   - Ⓐ $10.00
   - Ⓑ $100.00
   - Ⓒ $101.00

B Talk with a partner.

What are your classes?

2 Fun with vocabulary

A Talk with a partner. Read and match.

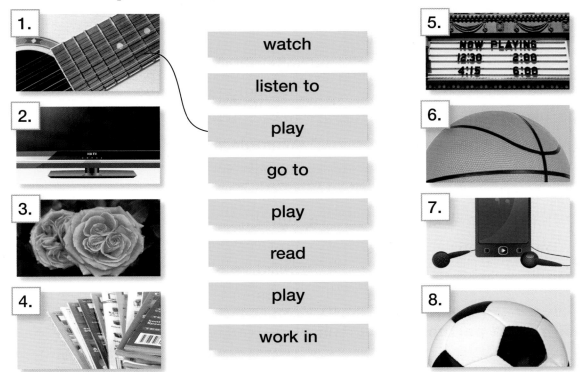

1.	watch	5.
2.	listen to	6.
3.	play	7.
4.	go to	8.
	play	
	read	
	play	
	work in	

B Talk with a partner. Complete the chart.

	Inside the house	Outside the house
cook	✓	✓
fish		
dance		
shop		
swim		
watch TV		

3 Wrap up

Complete the **Self-assessment** on page 145.

Review

1 Listening

CLASS CD2 TK 54

Read. Then listen and circle.

1. What is Marco doing?
   a. washing the car
   b. playing the guitar

2. What does he like to do?
   a. wash the car
   b. play the guitar

3. What is Ricky doing?
   a. making lunch
   b. making the bed

4. What is Fred doing?
   a. reading magazines
   b. watching TV

5. What does Tina like to do?
   a. cook
   b. exercise

6. What does she like to do on the weekend?
   a. fish
   b. dance

Talk with a partner. Ask and answer.

2 Vocabulary

Write. Complete the story.

| bedroom | kitchen | playing | watching | work |

Sunday at Home

Today is Sunday. My son is ___watching___ TV in the
                                    1
living room. My daughter is _____ the guitar in her
                                    2
_____ . My wife is in the _____ . She likes to
        3   4
cook. I am in the garden. I like to _____ in the garden.
                                          5
Sunday is our favorite day of the week. We like to relax.

3 Grammar

A Complete the sentences. Use *is* or *are*.

1. **A** What _____are_____ they doing?
   B Drying the dishes.

2. **A** What _____ she doing?
   B Taking out the trash.

3. **A** What _____ he doing?
   B Washing the clothes.

4. **A** What _____ they doing?
   B Getting the mail.

B Read and circle. Then write.

1. **A** What _____does_____ Pai like to do?
   do (does)

   B He _____ listen to music.
   like to   likes to

2. **A** What _____ Vance and Anh like to do?
   do   does

   B They _____ read magazines.
   like to   likes to

3. **A** What _____ you like to do?
   do   does

   B I _____ travel.
   like to   likes to

4 Pronunciation

A Listen to the two sounds of *a, e, i, o,* and *u.*

CLASS CD2 TK 55

a		e		i		o		u	
name	at	read	red	five	six	phone	on	June	bus

B Listen and repeat.

CLASS CD2 TK 56

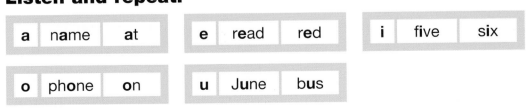

a	name	at

e	read	red

i	five	six

o	phone	on

u	June	bus

Talk with a partner. Say a word. Your partner points. Take turns.

Self-assessments

UNIT 1 Personal information

A Vocabulary Check (✓) the words you know.

☐ area code	☐ January	☐ July
☐ country	☐ February	☐ August
☐ first name	☐ March	☐ September
☐ ID card	☐ April	☐ October
☐ last name	☐ May	☐ November
☐ phone number	☐ June	☐ December

B Skills Check (✓) *Yes* or *No*.

	Yes	No
I can use **my**, **your**, **his**, and **her**: *What's **your** name?* **My** *name is Maria.*		
I can read about personal information.		
I can write about myself.		
I can read an ID card.		

C What's next? Choose one.

☐ I am ready for the unit test.

☐ I need more practice with _____ .

UNIT 2 At school

A Vocabulary Check (✓) the words you know.

☐ book   ☐ dictionary   ☐ pen
☐ chair   ☐ eraser   ☐ pencil
☐ computer   ☐ notebook   ☐ ruler
☐ desk   ☐ paper   ☐ stapler

B Skills Check (✓) *Yes* or *No*.

	Yes	No
I can use *in*, *on*, and *under*: *Where's my pencil?* **In** *the desk.* **On** *the desk.* **Under** *the desk.*		
I can read a note.		
I can write about school supplies.		
I can read a class schedule.		

C What's next? Choose one.

☐ I am ready for the unit test.
☐ I need more practice with _____ .

UNIT 3 Friends and family

A Vocabulary Check (✓) the words you know.

- ☐ aunt
- ☐ brother
- ☐ daughter
- ☐ father
- ☐ grandfather
- ☐ grandmother
- ☐ husband
- ☐ mother
- ☐ sister
- ☐ son
- ☐ uncle
- ☐ wife

B Skills Check (✓) Yes or No.

	Yes	No
I can ask and answer questions with **Do you have . . . ?**: **Do you have** a sister? **Yes, I do. No, I don't.**		
I can read about a family.		
I can write about my family.		
I can read a housing application.		

C What's next? Choose one.

- ☐ I am ready for the unit test.
- ☐ I need more practice with _____ .

UNIT 4 Health

A Vocabulary Check (✓) the words you know.

- ☐ arm
- ☐ cold
- ☐ eye
- ☐ fever
- ☐ foot
- ☐ hand
- ☐ head
- ☐ headache
- ☐ leg
- ☐ sore throat
- ☐ stomach
- ☐ toothache

B Skills Check (✓) Yes or No.

	Yes	No
I can use singular and plural nouns: **one eye**, **two eyes**		
I can read about health problems.		
I can complete a form.		
I can read a medicine label.		

C What's next? Choose one.

- ☐ I am ready for the unit test.
- ☐ I need more practice with _____ .

UNIT 5 Around town

A Vocabulary Check (✓) the words you know.

☐ bank	☐ library	☐ restaurant
☐ gas station	☐ movie theater	☐ school
☐ hospital	☐ pharmacy	☐ street
☐ laundromat	☐ post office	☐ supermarket

B Skills Check (✓) *Yes* or *No*.

	Yes	No
I can use **on**, **next to**, **across from**, and **between**: *Where's the school?* **Next to** *the bank.*		
I can read a notice about a new library.		
I can write about the buildings on a street.		
I can read a map.		

C What's next? Choose one.

☐ I am ready for the unit test.

☐ I need more practice with _____ .

UNIT 6 Time

A **Vocabulary** Check (✓) the words you know.

☐ appointment	☐ class	☐ meeting
☐ at midnight	☐ in the afternoon	☐ movie
☐ at night	☐ in the evening	☐ party
☐ at noon	☐ in the morning	☐ TV show

B **Skills** Check (✓) *Yes* or *No*.

	Yes	No
I can ask and answer *yes / no* questions with **be**: **Is** *your class at 11:00?* **Yes, it is. No, it isn't.**		
I can read about a schedule.		
I can write about my schedule.		
I can read an invitation.		

C **What's next?** Choose one.

☐ I am ready for the unit test.

☐ I need more practice with _____ .

UNIT 7 Shopping

A Vocabulary Check (✓) the words you know.

☐ blouse ☐ raincoat ☐ socks
☐ dress ☐ shirt ☐ sweater
☐ jacket ☐ shoes ☐ tie
☐ pants ☐ skirt ☐ T-shirt

B Skills Check (✓) *Yes* or *No*.

	Yes	No
I can ask questions with *How much*: *How much is* the shirt? *How much are* the shoes?		
I can read an e-mail.		
I can write a shopping list.		
I can read a receipt.		

C What's next? Choose one.

☐ I am ready for the unit test.
☐ I need more practice with _____ .

UNIT 8 Work

A **Vocabulary** Check (✓) the words you know.

☐ answer the phone	☐ custodian	☐ salesperson
☐ cashier	☐ fix cars	☐ sell clothes
☐ clean buildings	☐ mechanic	☐ serve food
☐ count money	☐ receptionist	☐ server

B **Skills** Check (✓) *Yes* or *No*.

	Yes	No
I can ask and answer questions with *does*: *Does* he *sell* clothes? *Yes*, he *does*. *No*, he *doesn't*.		
I can read an article about an employee.		
I can write about jobs.		
I can read a help-wanted ad.		

C **What's next?** Choose one.

☐ I am ready for the unit test.

☐ I need more practice with _____ .

UNIT 9 Daily living

A **Vocabulary** Check (✓) the words you know.

☐ cut the grass	☐ get the mail	☐ walk the dog
☐ do homework	☐ make lunch	☐ wash the car
☐ do the laundry	☐ make the bed	☐ wash the dishes
☐ dry the dishes	☐ take out the trash	☐ water the grass

B **Skills** Check (✓) *Yes* or *No*.

	Yes	No
I can ask and answer questions with **What**: **What is** he **doing**? **What are** they **doing**? **Making lunch.**		
I can read an e-mail about what people are doing.		
I can write about what people are doing.		
I can read a work order.		

C **What's next?** Choose one.

☐ I am ready for the unit test.

☐ I need more practice with _____ .

UNIT 10 Free time

A **Vocabulary** Check (✓) the words you know.

☐ cook	☐ listen to music	☐ read magazines
☐ dance	☐ play basketball	☐ swim
☐ exercise	☐ play cards	☐ watch TV
☐ fish	☐ play the guitar	☐ work in the garden

B **Skills** Check (✓) *Yes* or *No*.

	Yes	No
I can ask and answer questions with *like to*: *What **do** you **like to** do? I **like to** swim.*		
I can read an e-mail from a friend.		
I can write about what I like to do.		
I can read a course description.		

C **What's next?** Choose one.

☐ I am ready for the unit test.

☐ I need more practice with _____ .

Reference

Possessive adjectives

Questions

What's	my	phone number?
	your	
	his	
	her	
	its	
	our	
	your	
	their	

Answers

Your	phone number is 555-3348.
My	
His	
Her	
Its	
Your	
Our	
Their	

Present of *be*

Yes / No questions

Am	I	from Somalia?
Are	you	
Is	he	
Is	she	
Is	it	
Are	we	
Are	you	
Are	they	

Short answers

Yes,	you	are.
	I	am.
	he	is.
	she	is.
	it	is.
	you	are.
	we	are.
	they	are.

No,	you aren't.
	I'm not.
	he isn't.
	she isn't.
	it isn't.
	you aren't.
	we aren't.
	they aren't.

Contractions

I'm	=	I am
You're	=	You are
He's	=	He is
She's	=	She is
It's	=	It is
We're	=	We are
You're	=	You are
They're	=	They are

aren't	=	are not
isn't	=	is not

Simple present

Yes / No questions

Do	I	
Do	you	
Does	he	
Does	she	sell clothes?
Does	it	
Do	we	
Do	you	
Do	they	

Short answers

	you	do.
	I	do.
	he	does.
Yes,	she	does.
	it	does.
	you	do.
	we	do.
	they	do.

	you	don't.
	I	don't.
	he	doesn't.
No,	she	doesn't.
	it	doesn't.
	you	don't.
	we	don't.
	they	don't.

don't	=	do not
doesn't	=	does not

Present continuous

Questions with *What*

	am	I	
	are	you	
	is	he	
	is	she	
What	is	it	doing?
	are	we	
	are	you	
	are	they	

Short answers

Working.

Simple present of *like to* + verb

Questions with *What*

	do	I	
	do	you	
	does	he	
	does	she	
What	does	it	like to do?
	do	we	
	do	you	
	do	they	

Answers

You	like	
I	like	
He	likes	
She	likes	
It	likes	to swim.
You	like	
We	like	
They	like	

Yes / No questions

Do	I	
Do	you	
Does	he	
Does	she	like to swim?
Does	it	
Do	we	
Do	you	
Do	they	

Short answers

Yes,		
	you	do.
	I	do.
	he	does.
	she	does.
	it	does.
	you	do.
	we	do.
	they	do.

No,		
	you	don't.
	I	don't.
	he	doesn't.
	she	doesn't.
	it	doesn't.
	you	don't.
	we	don't.
	they	don't.

Simple present of *have*

Yes / No questions

Do	I	
Do	you	
Does	he	
Does	she	have a sister?
Do	we	
Do	you	
Do	they	

Short answers

Yes,		
	you	do.
	I	do.
	he	does.
	she	does.
	you	do.
	we	do.
	they	do.

No,		
	you	don't.
	I	don't.
	he	doesn't.
	she	doesn't.
	you	don't.
	we	don't.
	they	don't.

Affirmative statements

I	have	
You	have	
He	has	
She	has	a sister.
We	have	
You	have	
They	have	

Negative statements

I	don't		
You	don't		
He	doesn't		
She	doesn't	have	a sister.
We	don't		
You	don't		
They	don't		

Capitalization rules

Begin the first word in a sentence with a capital letter.	**M**y name is Nancy. **W**here is Ivan from?
Begin the names of months and days of the week with a capital letter.	**J**anuary **S**unday
Begin the names of countries, cities, streets, and other places with a capital letter.	**M**exico **F**lorida **T**ampa **P**ine **A**venue **T**he **C**lothes **P**lace
Begin the names of people with a capital letter.	**S**ara **G**arza **E**rnesto **D**elgado
Begin family relationship words with a capital when they are part of a name. Do not begin family relationship words with a capital when they are not part of a name.	I like **U**ncle Eduardo. My **u**ncle is Eduardo.
Begin a title with a capital when it is part of the name.	**M**rs. Navarro **D**r. Martin

Cardinal numbers

0 zero	10 ten	20 twenty	30 thirty	40 forty
1 one	11 eleven	21 twenty-one	31 thirty-one	50 fifty
2 two	12 twelve	22 twenty-two	32 thirty-two	60 sixty
3 three	13 thirteen	23 twenty-three	33 thirty-three	70 seventy
4 four	14 fourteen	24 twenty-four	34 thirty-four	80 eighty
5 five	15 fifteen	25 twenty-five	35 thirty-five	90 ninety
6 six	16 sixteen	26 twenty-six	36 thirty-six	100 one hundred
7 seven	17 seventeen	27 twenty-seven	37 thirty-seven	1,000 one thousand
8 eight	18 eighteen	28 twenty-eight	38 thirty-eight	
9 nine	19 nineteen	29 twenty-nine	39 thirty-nine	

Ordinal numbers

1st first	11th eleventh	21st twenty-first	31st thirty-first
2nd second	12th twelfth	22nd twenty-second	
3rd third	13th thirteenth	23rd twenty-third	
4th fourth	14th fourteenth	24th twenty-fourth	
5th fifth	15th fifteenth	25th twenty-fifth	
6th sixth	16th sixteenth	26th twenty-sixth	
7th seventh	17th seventeenth	27th twenty-seventh	
8th eighth	18th eighteenth	28th twenty-eighth	
9th ninth	19th nineteenth	29th twenty-ninth	
10th tenth	20th twentieth	30th thirtieth	

Metric equivalents

1 inch = 25 millimeters	1 dry ounce = 28 grams	1 fluid ounce = 30 milliliters
1 foot = 30 centimeters	1 pound = .45 kilograms	1 quart = .95 liters
1 yard = .9 meters	1 mile = 1.6 kilometers	1 gallon = 3.8 liters

Converting Farenheit temperatures to Celsius

Subtract 30 and divide by 2.
Example: 80°F − 30 = 50; divided by 2 = 25
80°F = approximately 25°C

Countries and nationalities

Afghanistan	Afghan	Germany	German	Portugal	Portuguese
Albania	Albanian	Ghana	Ghanaian	Puerto Rico	Puerto Rican
Algeria	Algerian	Greece	Greek	Republic of	Congolese
Angola	Angolan	Grenada	Grenadian	the Congo	
Argentina	Argentine	Guatemala	Guatemalan	Romania	Romanian
Armenia	Armenian	Guyana	Guyanese	Russia	Russian
Australia	Australian	Haiti	Haitian	Saudi Arabia	Saudi
Austria	Austrian	Herzegovina	Herzegovinian	Senegal	Senegalese
Azerbaijan	Azerbaijani	Honduras	Honduran	Serbia	Serbian
Bahamas	Bahamian	Hungary	Hungarian	Sierra Leone	Sierra Leonean
Bahrain	Bahraini	India	Indian	Singapore	Singaporean
Bangladesh	Bangladeshi	Indonesia	Indonesian	Slovakia	Slovak
Barbados	Barbadian	Iran	Iranian	Somalia	Somali
Belarus	Belarusian	Iraq	Iraqi	South Africa	South African
Belgium	Belgian	Ireland	Irish	South Korea	Korean
Belize	Belizean	Israel	Israeli	Spain	Spanish
Benin	Beninese	Italy	Italian	Sri Lanka	Sri Lankan
Bolivia	Bolivian	Jamaica	Jamaican	Sudan	Sudanese
Bosnia	Bosnian	Japan	Japanese	Sweden	Swedish
Brazil	Brazilian	Jordan	Jordanian	Switzerland	Swiss
Bulgaria	Bulgarian	Kazakhstan	Kazakhstani	Syria	Syrian
Cambodia	Cambodian	Kenya	Kenyan	Tajikistan	Tajikistani
Cameroon	Cameroonian	Kuwait	Kuwaiti	Tanzania	Tanzanian
Canada	Canadian	Laos	Laotian	Thailand	Thai
Cape Verde	Cape Verdean	Lebanon	Lebanese	Togo	Togolese
Chile	Chilean	Liberia	Liberian	Tonga	Tongan
China	Chinese	Lithuania	Lithuanian	Trinidad	Trinidadian
Colombia	Colombian	Macedonia	Macedonian	Tunisia	Tunisian
Comoros	Comoran	Malaysia	Malaysian	Turkey	Turkish
Costa Rica	Costa Rican	Mexico	Mexican	Turkmenistan	Turkmen
Côte d'Ivoire	Ivoirian	Morocco	Moroccan	Uganda	Ugandan
Croatia	Croatian	Myanmar	Myanmar	Ukraine	Ukrainian
Cuba	Cuban	(Burma)	(Burmese)	United Arab	Emirati
Dominica	Dominican	Nepal	Nepali	Emirates	
Dominican	Dominican	Netherlands	Dutch	United	British
Republic		New Zealand	New Zealander	Kingdom	
Ecuador	Ecuadorian	Nicaragua	Nicaraguan	United States	American
Egypt	Egyptian	Niger	Nigerien	Uruguay	Uruguayan
El Salvador	Salvadoran	Nigeria	Nigerian	Uzbekistan	Uzbekistani
Equatorial	Equatorial	Norway	Norwegian	Venezuela	Venezuelan
Guinea	Guinean	Pakistan	Pakistani	Vietnam	Vietnamese
Eritrea	Eritrean	Panama	Panamanian	Yemen	Yemeni
Ethiopia	Ethiopian	Paraguay	Paraguayan	Zambia	Zambian
Fiji	Fijian	Peru	Peruvian	Zimbabwe	Zimbabwean
France	French	Philippines	Filipino		
Georgia	Georgian	Poland	Polish		

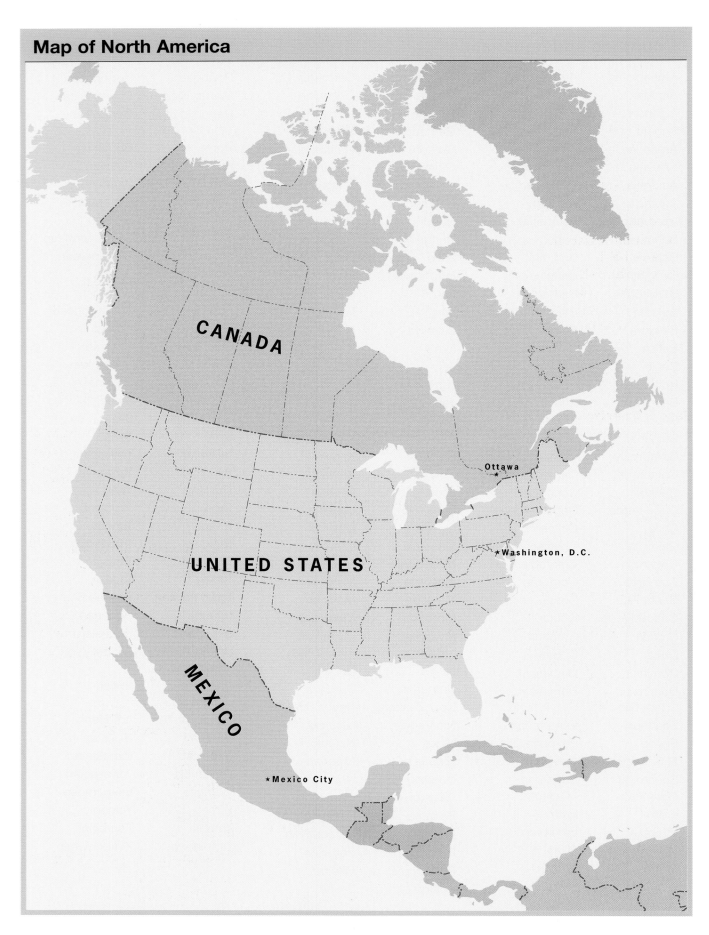

CANADA

Ottawa
★

UNITED STATES

★Washington, D.C.

MEXICO

★Mexico City

Self-study audio script

Welcome

Page 3, Exercise 2A – Track 2
A, B, C, D, E, F, G, H, I, J, K, L, M, N, O, P, Q, R, S, T, U, V, W, X, Y, Z

Page 3, Exercise 2B – Track 3
1. Hello, my name is Anita.
   A-N-I-T-A.
2. My name is Daniel.
   D-A-N-I-E-L.
3. I'm Peizhi. P-E-I-Z-H-I.
4. My name is Yuri. Y-U-R-I.
5. Hi, I'm Franco. F-R-A-N-C-O.
6. Hi, my name is Lee. L-E-E.
7. Hello, my name is Hakim.
   H-A-K-I-M.
8. Hi there. My name is Karla.
   K-A-R-L-A.

Page 4, Exercise 3A – Track 4
1. Look.
2. Listen.
3. Point.
4. Repeat.
5. Talk.
6. Write.
7. Read.
8. Circle.
9. Match.

Page 5, Exercise 4A – Track 5
One, two, three, four, five, six, seven, eight, nine, ten, eleven, twelve, thirteen, fourteen, fifteen, sixteen, seventeen, eighteen, nineteen, twenty

Page 5, Exercise 4B – Track 6
1. six
2. eighteen
3. five
4. three
5. twelve
6. eleven
7. fifteen
8. nine

Unit 1: Personal information

Page 7, Exercise 2A – Track 7
1. area code
2. country
3. first name
4. ID card
5. last name
6. phone number

Page 7, Exercise 2B – Track 8
1. A What's your area code?
   B 201.
2. A What's your phone number?
   B 555-5983.
3. A What's your first name?
   B Glen.
4. A What's your last name?
   B Reyna.

Page 12, Exercise 2 – Track 9
Welcome!
   Meet our new student. His first name is Ernesto. His last name is Delgado. He is from Mexico. Welcome, Ernesto Delgado!

Page 13, Exercise 4A – Track 10
1. January
2. February
3. March
4. April
5. May
6. June
7. July
8. August
9. September
10. October
11. November
12. December

Unit 2: At school

Page 19, Exercise 2A – Track 11
1. a book
2. a chair
3. a computer
4. a desk
5. a notebook
6. a pencil

Page 19, Exercise 2B – Track 12
1. A What do you need?
   B A pencil.
   A Here. Take this one.
2. A What do you need?
   B A notebook.
   A Here. Take this one.
3. A What do you need?
   B A book.
   A Here. Take this one.
4. A What do you need?
   B A chair.
   A Here. Take this one.

Page 24, Exercise 2 – Track 13
Sue,

   It's Monday, your first day of English class! You need a pencil, eraser, notebook, and dictionary. The pencil is in the desk. The eraser is on the desk. The notebook is on my computer. And the dictionary is under the chair. Have fun at school!

   Mom

Page 25, Exercise 4A – Track 14
1. Monday
2. Tuesday
3. Wednesday
4. Thursday
5. Friday
6. Saturday
7. Sunday

Unit 3: Friends and family

Page 33, Exercise 2A – Track 15
1. daughter
2. father
3. grandfather
4. grandmother
5. mother
6. son

Page 33, Exercise 2B – Track 16
1. A Who's that?
   B The grandmother.

2. **A** Who's that?
   B The daughter.
3. **A** Who's that?
   B The father.
4. **A** Who's that?
   B The grandfather.

Page 38, Exercise 2 – Track 17

My Family

My name is Gloria. This is my family. This is my mother. Her name is Natalia. It is her birthday. This is my father. His name is Enrico. This is my husband, Luis. We have one daughter. Her name is Lisa. We have one son. His name is Tony. I love my family!

Page 39, Exercise 4A – Track 18

1. baby
2. girl
3. boy
4. teenager
5. woman
6. man

Unit 4: Health

Page 45, Exercise 2A – Track 19

1. doctor
2. doctor's office
3. medicine
4. nurse
5. patient

Page 45, Exercise 2B – Track 20

1. **A** What's the matter?
   B I need a nurse.
2. **A** What's the matter?
   B I need a doctor.
3. **A** What's the matter?
   B I need a nurse.
4. **A** What's the matter?
   B I need some medicine.

Page 50, Exercise 2 – Track 21

At the Doctor's Office

Tony and Mario are at the doctor's office. They are patients. Tony's leg hurts. His head hurts, too. He has a headache. Mario's arm hurts. His hands hurt, too. Tony and Mario are not happy. It is not a good day.

Page 51, Exercise 4A – Track 22

1. a cold
2. a fever
3. a headache
4. a sore throat
5. a stomachache
6. a toothache

Unit 5: Around town

Page 59, Exercise 2A – Track 23

1. bank
2. library
3. restaurant
4. school
5. street
6. supermarket

Page 59, Exercise 2B – Track 24

1. **A** Where's the school?
   B The school? It's on Main Street.
   A Thanks.
2. **A** Where's the restaurant?
   B The restaurant? I don't know.
   A OK. Thank you.
3. **A** Where's the library?
   B The library's on Market Street.
   A Thanks a lot.
4. **A** Where's the supermarket?
   B Sorry, I don't know.
   A Thanks, anyway.

Page 64, Exercise 2 – Track 25

Notice from Riverside Library

Come and visit Riverside Library. The new library opens today. The library is on Main Street. It is across from Riverside Adult School. It is next to K and P Supermarket. It is between K and P Supermarket and Rosie's Restaurant. The library is open from 9:00 to 5:00, Monday, Wednesday, and Friday.

Page 65, Exercise 4A – Track 26

1. by bicycle
2. by bus
3. by car
4. by taxi

5. by train
6. on foot

Unit 6: Time

Page 71, Exercise 2A – Track 27

1. seven o'clock
2. nine o'clock
3. ten o'clock
4. ten-thirty
5. two-thirty
6. six-thirty

Page 71, Exercise 2B – Track 28

1. **A** What time is it?
   B It's nine o'clock.
2. **A** Excuse me. What time is it?
   B It's ten-thirty.
3. **A** What time is it?
   B It's two-thirty.
4. **A** Excuse me. What time is it?
   B It's ten o'clock.

Page 76, Exercise 2 – Track 29

Teresa's Day

Teresa is busy today. Her meeting with her friend Joan is at 10:00 in the morning. Her doctor's appointment is at 1:00 in the afternoon. Her favorite TV show is at 4:30. Her class is at 6:30 in the evening. Her uncle's birthday party is also at 6:30. Oh, no! What will she do?

Page 77, Exercise 4A – Track 30

1. in the morning
2. in the afternoon
3. in the evening
4. at noon
5. at night
6. at midnight

Unit 7: Shopping

Page 85, Exercise 2A – Track 31

1. a dress   4. shoes
2. pants   5. socks
3. a shirt   6. a T-shirt

Page 85, Exercise 2B – Track 32

1. **A** How much is the shirt?
   B The shirt? Nineteen dollars.
2. **A** How much are the socks?
   B The socks? One ninety-nine.

3. **A** How much is the dress?
   B The dress? Thirty-nine ninety-nine.
4. **A** How much are the pants?
   B The pants? Twenty-four ninety-nine.

Page 90, Exercise 2 – Track 33

Hi Patty,

This morning, Samuel and I are going to The Clothes Place. Samuel needs blue pants. He needs a tie, too. I need a red dress and black shoes. Dresses are on sale. They're $49.99. Shoes are on sale, too. They're $34.99. That's good.

Call you later,
Rose

Page 91, Exercise 4A – Track 34

1. black
2. white
3. yellow
4. orange
5. brown
6. green
7. blue
8. purple
9. pink
10. red

Unit 8: Work

Page 97, Exercise 2A – Track 35

1. cashier
2. custodian
3. mechanic
4. receptionist
5. salesperson
6. server

Page 97, Exercise 2B – Track 36

1. **A** What does he do?
   B He's a server.
2. **A** What does she do?
   B She's a receptionist.
3. **A** What's his job?
   B He's a custodian.
4. **A** What's her job?
   B She's a mechanic.

Page 102, Exercise 2 – Track 37

Employee of the Month:
Sara Lopez
   Congratulations, Sara Lopez – Employee of the Month! Sara is a salesperson. She sells clothes. Sara's whole family works here at Shop Smart. Her father is a custodian, and her mother is a receptionist. Her Uncle Eduardo is a server. He serves food. Her sister Lucy is a cashier. She counts money. Her brother Leo fixes cars. He's a mechanic. Everybody in the store knows the Lopez family!

Page 103, Exercise 4A – Track 38

1. bus driver
2. homemaker
3. painter
4. plumber
5. teacher's aide
6. truck driver

Unit 9: Daily living

Page 111, Exercise 2A – Track 39

1. doing homework
2. doing the laundry
3. drying the dishes
4. making lunch
5. making the bed
6. washing the dishes

Page 111, Exercise 2B – Track 40

1. **A** What's she doing?
   B She's doing homework.
2. **A** What's he doing?
   B He's washing the dishes.
3. **A** What's she doing?
   B She's making the bed.
4. **A** What's he doing?
   B He's making lunch.

Page 116, Exercise 2 – Track 41

Dear Susie,

It's after dinner. My family is working in the kitchen. My daughter Li is washing the dishes. My daughter Mei is drying the dishes. My husband and Tao are taking out the trash. Where is my oldest son? He isn't in the kitchen. He is sleeping in the living room! I am not happy.

I need help. What can I do?

Huan

Page 117, Exercise 4A – Track 42

1. bathroom
2. bedroom
3. living room
4. laundry room
5. kitchen
6. dining room

Unit 10: Free time

Page 123, Exercise 2A – Track 43

1. dance
2. exercise
3. fish
4. play basketball
5. play cards
6. swim

Page 123, Exercise 2B – Track 44

1. **A** Do you like to dance?
   B Yes, we do.
2. **A** Do you like to play cards?
   B Yes, we do.
3. **A** What do you like to do?
   B I like to fish.
4. **A** What do you like to do?
   B I like to swim.

Page 128, Exercise 2 – Track 45

Hi Miriam,

I'm not working today. It's my day off. Are you busy? Come and visit me!

What do you like to do? I like to cook. I like to play cards. I like to listen to music and dance. I like to watch TV. Do you like to watch TV?

Please call me at 10:00.

See you soon!

Lupe

Page 129, Exercise 4A – Track 46

1. go to the movies
2. go online
3. shop
4. travel
5. visit friends
6. volunteer

Illustration credits

Photography credits

Track (STUDENT TK) Listing for Self-Study Audio CD

Track	Page	Exercise
1		
2	3	2A
3	3	2B
4	4	3A
5	5	4A
6	5	4B
7	7	2A
8	7	2B
9	12	2
10	13	4A
11	19	2A
12	19	2B
13	24	2
14	25	4A
15	33	2A
16	33	2B

Track	Page	Exercise
17	38	2
18	39	4A
19	45	2A
20	45	2B
21	50	2
22	51	4A
23	59	2A
24	59	2B
25	64	2
26	65	4A
27	71	2A
28	71	2B
29	76	2
30	77	4A
31	85	2A

Track	Page	Exercise
32	85	2B
33	90	2
34	91	4A
35	97	2A
36	97	2B
37	102	2
38	103	4A
39	111	2A
40	111	2B
41	116	2
42	117	4A
43	123	2A
44	123	2B
45	128	2
46	129	4A